THE ANCESTRAL CONSTITUTION

THE
ANCESTRAL CONSTITUTION

FOUR STUDIES
IN ATHENIAN PARTY POLITICS
AT THE END
OF THE FIFTH CENTURY B.C.

by

ALEXANDER FUKS

GREENWOOD PRESS, PUBLISHERS
WESTPORT, CONNECTICUT

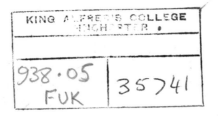
PATRI OPTIMO SACRUM

Originally published in 1953
by Routledge & Kegan Paul, Ltd., London

Reprinted with the permission
of Routledge & Kegan Paul, Ltd.

First Greenwood Reprinting 1971

Library of Congress Catalogue Card Number 72-138235

ISBN 0-8371-5592-4

Printed in the United States of America

PREFACE

THE return to the 'ancestral constitution' was in
411–403 B.C. a major issue in Athenian politics.
The scope and import of this party-political
issue is here made the subject of a special study. The
commonly held view is that each of the three groups
in Athenian politics—the oligarchs, the moderates and
the democrats—propounded its own version of the 'ancestral constitution'. This is not borne out by an examination of the relevant evidence. Such an examination
seems to show that the launching of the slogan of πάτριος
πολιτεία, and the employment of the argument from the
constitutional past for political purposes of the day, were
particularly connected with the moderate group in Athenian politics. This study of the πάτριος πολιτεία is, consequently, mainly an enquiry about the moderate group.
It involves discussion of several aspects of the moderate
thought and propaganda other than πάτριος πολιτεία,
though it does not purport to be a full and systematic
exposition of the moderate programme.

My first chapter is a discussion of the knotty problem of

v

the Rider of Kleitophon. An attempt is made to elucidate Kleitophon's amendment with the help of the views of the Theramenean group, and of the moderate fourth-century tradition of Athens' early constitutional history. My excuse for the rather excessive length of that discussion is that Kleitophon's Rider seems to be the best clue to the understanding of the moderates' call for a 'return to the ancestral constitution', and to their views on Athens' earlier constitutional history, especially on the work of Solon and Kleisthenes. Chapter II discusses the use of the term πάτριος πολιτεία by the democrats. The evidence brought forth in it seems to lead to the conclusion that π.π. never was for the democrats a far-off good constitution to be striven after. Though they sometimes used the expression π.π., it denoted for them democracy as it stood. The third chapter is devoted to a study of the employment of the slogan of the 'ancestral constitution' in the period 404–403 B.C. The evidence discussed seems to show that it was then, perhaps even more than in 411, a crucial point in the propaganda of the moderates. My last enquiry deals with the much discussed question of the mysterious 'constitution of Drakon'. The suggestion put forward is that the 'constitution of Drakon' stems from moderate fourth-century re-interpretation of Athens' early constitutional history, not from party-political clashes of the late fifth century. If this is correct, the 'constitution of Drakon' rounds off the delineation of the fourth-century tradition given in Chapter I.

I am much indebted to Professor H. T. Wade-Gery who has been good enough to read and criticize my manuscript. My colleague, Dr Ch. Wirszubski, I should like to thank for some useful discussion. My thanks are also due to the Zangwill Memorial Trust and to the Society of English Friends of the Hebrew University for their financial assistance.

A. F.

The Hebrew University, Jerusalem
September 1952

vii

CONTENTS

ix

Chapter I

THE RIDER OF KLEITOPHON
AND THE TRADITION OF
SOLON AND KLEISTHENES

Aﬀ FTER having recounted the proposal of Pythodoros
to choose thirty συγγραφεῖς for revision of Athens'
constitution, Aristotle continues: Κλειτοφῶν δὲ τὰ
μὲν ἄλλα καθάπερ Πυθόδωρος εἶπεν, προσαναζητῆσαι δὲ τοὺς
αἱρεθέντας ἔγραψεν καὶ τοὺς πατρίους νόμους οὓς Κλεισθένης
ἔθηκεν ὅτε καθίστη τὴν δημοκρατίαν, ὅπως <ἂν> ἀκούσαντες καὶ
τούτων βουλεύσωνται τὸ ἄριστον, ὡς οὐ δημοτικὴν ἀλλὰ παρα-
πλησίαν οὖσαν τὴν Κλεισθένους πολιτείαν τῇ Σόλωνος . . . Ath.
Pol. 29,3.

The technical language in which this proposal is introduced [1] supports the widely accepted supposition that the
account in the Ath. Pol. is based on the Rider of
Kleitophon. There seems, however, to be a discrepancy
between the qualification after the name of Kleisthenes
'when he created the democracy', and the motivation (or
explanation) 'since the constitution of Kleisthenes was not
democratic, but closely akin to that of Solon'. Although
Kleitophon's amendment has been frequently mentioned

in connection with the events of 411, this difficulty seems to have been tackled only by Wade-Gery, *C.Q.* 27 (1933), pp. 19 sqq., and Munro, *C.Q.* 33 (1939), pp. 84 sqq.

According to Munro the ὡς . . . *Σόλωνος* clause is Aristotle's addition; it is both an explanation of Kleitophon's reasons and a criticism of them, since according to Aristotle the constitution of Kleisthenes was not akin to that of Solon, but in fact Aristotle was wrong, Kleitophon right. Kleisthenes was, according to Munro's hypothesis, author of three consecutive constitutions. Only the last of these was democratic. Kleitophon refers to the first and the second which were undemocratic in character. The *καθίστη* . . . *δημοκρατίαν* of Kleitophon is an ironical expression calculated to pique the democrats.

Unless the use of irony is better attested in Athenian decrees we shall have to disregard its alleged occurrence in Kleitophon's Rider; also, we shall have to reject Munro's multiplication of Kleisthenes' constitutions, stick to the sources in hand—which are disregarded by Munro—and look elsewhere for explanation of Kleitophon's Rider.

According to Wade-Gery, *ὅτε* . . . *δημοκρατίαν* belongs to the text of the Rider; *ὡς* . . . *Σόλωνος* is an explanation, which derives from Aristotle's source. This source was Antiphon's Defence speech. Kleitophon was a moderate-oligarch, Kleisthenes' constitution basically democratic. Kleitophon could not, therefore, have recommended Kleisthenes' constitution. The real purpose of Kleitophon was to point out the procedure of revolutionizing the state by

2

the use of psephismata. Kleitophon wanted the opposition in 411 to follow Kleisthenes' technique, not his constitution. This does not seem to fit in with the explanation, allegedly Antiphon's, of Kleitophon's proposal. The Solon clause, whatever its exact meaning, is concerned with Kleisthenes' constitution (Κλεισθένους πολιτείαν), not with his procedure. Nor does it seem to me to be demonstrable that Antiphon's speech was here the source of Aristotle (Androtion has again been urged recently by Jacoby, *Atthis*, 1949, p. 384, n. 30). If my following argument (pp. 4 sqq.) is correct it would appear that there is no need to invoke Antiphon, and to suppose that Kleitophon was concerned with Kleisthenes' technique, in order to explain Kleitophon's Rider.[2]

Kleitophon is mentioned in *Ath. Pol.* 34,3 as one of the supporters of Theramenes striving to establish the 'ancestral constitution' at Athens;[3] he is coupled with Theramenes also in Aristoph. *Ran.* 967, and there can be little doubt that he was a moderate, and his Rider a proposal of the Theramenean group.[4]

The question is whether the words ὅτε . . . δημοκρατίαν could have been included in a moderate motion, and if so how they could be compatible with the motivation ὡς οὐ δημοτικὴν κτλ.

If we suppose Kleitophon's meaning to be that Kleisthenes was the creator of the Athenian democracy in the sense of the constitution of his own time, his views would be here identical with those of the democrats. By the time

3

Herodotos wrote his *History*, Kleisthenes was already established as the creator of the democratic constitution. He is called by Herodotos: ὁ τὰς φυλὰς καὶ τὴν δημοκρατίην καταστήσας (6,131,1).[5] This was the official view of the Periclean democracy.[6] The Athenian democrats claimed—at least as early as about a generation before 411—that *their democracy* was created by Kleisthenes. However, it is scarcely credible that it is the official democratic view which Kleitophon puts forward in his Rider. Furthermore, the search for Kleisthenes' constitution, recommended by the Rider, would be meaningless on that supposition—to the democrats their constitution as it stood was established by Kleisthenes (see also below, pp. 33 sqq.); and the motivation clause would hardly be intelligible.

It seems to me, however, that Kleitophon's Rider may be explained on the supposition that it embodies the views of the moderates, and that on this supposition there is no discrepancy between the ὅτε . . . δημοκρατίαν and the Solon clause.

Whatever the name the moderates wanted their regime to be called by (cf. below, pp. 8 sqq.), their slogan before the establishment of the Four Hundred seems to have been μὴ τὸν αὐτὸν τρόπον δημοκρατεῖσθαι, not μὴ δημοκρατεῖσθαι.[7] It is a demand for a change of the unrestricted contemporary democracy, not for abolition of democracy as such. This slogan is reported by Thukydides to have been propounded by οἱ μετὰ τοῦ Πεισάνδρου πρέσβεις, but there seems to be little doubt that the propaganda before the

4

establishment of the Four Hundred, and in the first stage
of their rule, was conducted on moderate lines, and that
several of the arguments of the moderates were used in
the Assembly in which this slogan was launched.[8] We have
to reckon with the possibility that propagandist motives
might have influenced the coining of this catchword, but
even in this case it would seem to follow that the
moderates did not shun the very name of democracy (as
the oligarchs, cf. e.g. Thuc. 8,92,11, did [9]), although they
would understand by it something different from the
extreme democracy of their time. Evidence drawn from
Isokrates seems to strengthen this supposition. Isokrates
was influenced by the views of the Theramenean group,
and he supported a somewhat similar trend in contemporary politics.[10] Although he criticized the democracy of
Kleitophon's time,[11] as did the Therameneans, and was
strongly opposed to the democratic regime of his own
day,[12] he recommends the 'Kleisthenean democracy' as
Kleitophon did. This 'democracy established by Kleisthenes'[13] is for him always ἐκείνη ἡ δημοκρατία (as opposed
to the ἡ κακῶς καθεστηκυῖα δημοκρατία), the 'good old constitution of the forefathers' perverted by its later supporters,
the 'true democracy',[14] which has little in common with
demagogy and mob-rule as they developed in the late fifth
and in the fourth centuries.[15] It is used, I suggest, in the
same sense in Kleitophon's Rider. If the 'democracy'
spoken of in the Rider needs research to be found out, if
Kleisthenes' were the 'ancestral laws' to be striven after,

5

.. δημοκρατίαν clause is a criticism of con-
mocracy. It is, I suggest, a case in point in
tical rivalry for re-interpretation of Athens'
history, which we shall have the opportunity
.... in some detail (below, pp. 7 sqq., 95 sqq.). It seems
that by 411 (and possibly before that date) the moderates
realized that Kleisthenes' constitution was not democratic
in the sense common in late fifth-century politics, but con-
tained some features on which their projected constitution
could be modelled; also, that they here possessed a weapon
of party-political propaganda which could be used against
the democrats.[16]

If this is correct the Solon clause would seem to become
compatible with the main clause of Kleitophon's Rider. It
gives the motivation of Kleitophon's proposal. It is doubtful whether this clause as it stands could have been included
in the Rider. Its wording does not fit in with the phraseo-
logy of decrees; it seems to be syntactically an appended
sentence, and ἄριστον (cf. *Ath. Pol.* 29,2) appears to have
been the final word of the decree. It is, however, not impossible that some statement to the effect that Kleisthenes'
'ancestral constitution' was not really democratic but akin
to that of Solon was included in the original amendment.
Aristotle may well have taken it out from its context and
have related it in his own words as an explanation of
Kleitophon's main point.[17] It would be idle to guess what
was its original form; but motivation is not unknown to
Athenian decrees,[18] and the possibility that a motivation,

6

the general trend of which is reproduced in the Solon clause, was included in the Rider is to be reckoned with. Another possibility is that this motivation was included in a speech made by Kleitophon, or by one of his associates before the Rider was moved.[19] The latter seems the more probable. A controversial motivation if included in the decree would seem to prejudge the search, while some such statement as: 'enquire, and this is the answer I am sure you will get' would be quite reasonable in a speech. Even if we set aside the above possibilities and suppose that ὡς . . . Σόλωνος is Aristotle's own explanation of Kleitophon's main clause and is not directly based on documentary evidence it may still be regarded as giving the correct reasons for Kleitophon's proposal. The view expressed in this clause is decidedly opposed to that held by Aristotle himself. To him the constitution of Kleisthenes was not at all akin to that of Solon but on the contrary 'much more democratic than that of Solon' (*Ath. Pol.* 22,1).[20] This seems to me to enhance the evidential value of the Solon clause and to support a supposition that Aristotle may be explaining here Kleitophon's Rider on the basis of what he knew of the constitutional views of Kleitophon, or of the Therameneans in general.

The views expressed in the motivation tally again with those of Isokrates. Isokrates' political ideal was a restoration of Athens' glorious past; revival of the virtues of the past generations was to him a panacea for all the evils of the present. His language is often vague, and the glorious ancestors to be imitated are shrouded in somewhat mythological mists, but there is little doubt that the 'ancestral constitution' (πατρία διοίκησις) to be striven for is to him in the main the constitution of Solon re-established by Kleisthenes.[21] There is no differentiation between the Solonian and the Kleisthenean constitutions to be found in Isokrates; and his repeated statement that Kleisthenes re-established the polity of Solon [22] is clearly based on the view that the Kleisthenean constitution was 'closely akin to that of Solon'.[23]

The constitution of Kleisthenes is spoken of in Plut. *Pericl.* 3,2 as πολιτεία ἄριστα κεκραμένη πρὸς ὁμόνοιαν καὶ σωτηρίαν, that is, a 'mixed-constitution'. This is in accord with the views of the Theramenean group, and those of Isokrates, and together with them throws some light on Kleitophon's Rider. A mixed-moderate constitution was an ideal of the Theramenean group; it appears as a middle course between democracy and oligarchy in Theramenes' speech in the *Hellenika*; it is a μετρία ξύγκρασις for Thukydides, and a μέση πολιτεία for Aristotle.[24] For Isokrates the 'good democracy of yore' (ἐκείνη, or ἀληθὴς δημοκρατία) is clearly a constitution of the right blend of different elements.[25]

In Plut. *Cim.* 15,1-3 the reforms of Ephialtes are regarded as a change of the 'ancestral constitution' (τῆς πολιτείας κόσμον τά ⟨τε⟩ πάτρια νόμιμα . . . ἀφείλοντο),[26] and Kimon's endeavours to stem these developments are described as a fight against extreme democracy. Kimon's

8

aim was, according to the source of Plutarch, to revive the 'aristocratic constitution of Kleisthenes' time' (τὴν ἐπὶ Κλεισθένους ἐγείρειν ἀριστοκρατίαν).[27] This seems to belong to the trend of tradition which manifests itself in Isokrates and in Plut. *Pericl.* 3,2, and originally derives, I suggest, from the group responsible for Kleitophon's Rider. The constitution before the reforms of 462-1, i.e. basically the Kleisthenean, is ,to the tradition represented in *Cim.* 15, 1-3 'ancestral laws', as it is both in Kleitophon's Rider and in Isokrates. The constitution of Kleisthenes is described in Plut. *Cim.* 15,1-3 as ἀριστοκρατία; it is an ἄριστα κεκραμένη πολιτεία in Plut. *Pericl.* 3,2; according to the Rider and to Isokrates Kleisthenes established a 'true democracy' akin to the constitution of Solon, and not at all democratic in the current sense. But the differences are differences of nomenclature not of substance or spirit. Both Kleitophon and Isokrates operate with the term *demokratia*, although they state clearly their opposition to 'the democracy of the democrats'. We have, however, some evidence which seems to show that both the fifth-century moderates and Isokrates—whether they believed that the constitution envisaged by them was the 'true democracy' or not—had good reasons of political propaganda and expediency for using the term *demokratia*. However, they seem to have been aware that their ideal was in some of its features close to an *aristokratia*, and possibly occasionally used the latter term. According to Isokrates, Lykurgos modelled the Spartan constitution on the 'ancestral polity' of Athens.

9

This ancient constitution of Athens which was, allegedly, Lykurgos' model, and, undoubtedly, Isokrates' ideal, was to him: δημοκρατία . . . ἡ ἀριστοκρατίᾳ μεμιγμένη . . XII, 153, a form of government close to the ἀπὸ τιμημάτων πολιτεία (XII, 131). His ideal was a kind of aristocratically ruled popular state (δημοκρατία . . . ἀριστοκρατίᾳ χρωμένη XII, 131), and he never wearies of stressing the importance of election ἐκ προκρίτων of really qualified citizens in the 'ancestral constitution', and of demanding for Athens an aristocratic leadership of the καλοὶ κἀγαθοί.[28] In XII, 132–3, he attempts to explain the reason why he does not apply the term aristokratia to his political ideal. There are only three basic forms of constitutions; aristocracy is not one of them. What really counts is the quality of leadership in each of them. But it looks as if he arrived here at this classification because operating with the term demokratia was both safer for personal reasons and politically more expedient. Isokrates' purpose was to exert political influence, and for an opposition pamphleteer under the democratic regime a cautious choice of suitable terms and slogans was not unimportant. Nor are reasons of a more personal nature to be disregarded. Isokrates knew well enough that his trenchant criticism of the Athenian democracy would evoke the usual accusation of oligarchic sympathies, and he rather laboriously stressed—in the Areopagitikos for example [29]—his loyalty to democracy and his strong opposition to the oligarchic regime. The case of 'ancestral constitution' seems to be characteristic of Isokrates' cautious choice of terms, and his susceptibility to possible attacks. A πάτριος πολιτεία is one of his main political themes, but this, perhaps somewhat discredited, slogan is carefully avoided in his writings. The 'ancestral constitution' is sometimes called πατρία διοίκησις, sometimes paraphrased in yet other terms—never πάτριος πολιτεία.[30] Isokrates quotes at length in the Antidosis speech the advice he had often given to his pupil and friend Timotheos which comes to the advisability of pleasing the general democratic public (XV, 132). This maxim of ἐπιχαρίτως λέγειν was lost on Timotheos; but it was observed by Isokrates himself, and seems to explain something of his political terminology. The case of the Theramenean group is partly not dissimilar, and it has more direct bearing on Kleitophon's Rider. The moderates, a constitutionalist party opposed to rule by force (βιαία ἀρχή) of the oligarchs, were dependent upon political propaganda more than were the oligarchic 'activists'.[31] They spoke cautiously of μετακινεῖν τὴν πολιτείαν, ἐπανορθοῦν τὴν πολιτείαν, and of μὴ τὸν αὐτὸν τρόπον δημοκρατεῖσθαι.[32] Whatever the name they wanted their constitution to be called by, the effect of such a slogan as 'the good old democracy of Kleisthenes' on, say, the upper strata of the supporters of the democratic regime might have been considerable. For Aristotle their polity would come under the generic name of *politeia*,[33] but there is no indication that it was thus called by the Therameneans themselves. It has been suggested, with some plausibility I believe, that in the rejection of the overtures of the

Athenian opposition by Thasos (Thuc. 8,64,3) a political slogan used by the Athenians is played upon.[34] On the eve of the revolution of 411 a change of the democratic constitution of Thasos was effected by the Athenian Diitrephes in accordance with the opposition's plan of suppressing the democratic regime in the cities of the empire. It is reported by Thukydides (l.c.) that shortly afterwards the Thasians fortified their city: ὡς τῆς μὲν μετ᾽ Ἀθηναίων ἀριστοκρατίας οὐδὲν ἔτι προσδεόμενοι τὴν δ᾽ ἀπὸ Λακεδαιμονίων ἐλευθερίαν ὁσημέραι προσδεχόμενοι (cf. 8,64,5). Possibly the slogan of 'aristocratic government for the allies' is here tauntingly thrown back at the Athenians, and it would seem to suit the moderates' attitude towards the cities of the empire.[35] Whether it was occasionally propounded to the Athenian public we do not know for certain.[36] It seems, however, that a writer who was in sympathy with the views of the moderates, and shared their opinions of Kleisthenes, but was not influenced by reasons of propaganda and expediency—as were both the Therameneans and Isokrates—might well have spoken of an 'aristocracy of Kleisthenes' as does the source of Plut. *Cim.* 15,1–3.[37] It seems to me that the tradition embodied in *Cim.* 15,1–3, and in *Pericl.* 3,2, comes from such a writer, or writers. The interest taken by the *Atthidographers* in Kleisthenes' work is well known,[38] and the inclusion of the Atthidographic tradition in some of Plutarch's Athenian lives is generally recognized, while its existence in *Cim.* 15,1–3 seems to have been proved by Ed. Meyer.[39] In view of this I venture to suggest that the tradition of Kleisthenes' 'mixed' or 'aristocratic' constitution stems from one, or more, of the conservative Atthidographers; [40] and that this conservative tradition helps, together with the views of the Theramenean group, and some of Isokrates' opinions, to elucidate the place of Kleisthenes in Kleitophon's Rider.

Two additional points are to be borne in mind; firstly, the language of the Rider is fairly precise—it does not advocate the re-establishment of Kleisthenes' constitution to the letter, but only recommends taking into account the political laws of Kleisthenes when the constitutional problems of the present are tackled. Secondly, research among documents and scrutiny of Kleisthenes' 'ancestral laws' is recommended *because* his constitution is supposed to have been akin to that of Solon. Whether Solon was mentioned in the Rider or in the introductory speech, he seems to have been for Kleitophon's group at least as important a figure as Kleisthenes. However, it is the 'ancestral laws' of Kleisthenes not of Solon for which a search among documents is to be undertaken. If Kleitophon believed—as Isokrates did, or anyway said he did—that there was practically no difference between the constitutions of Solon and Kleisthenes [41] this would become understandable. It is also possible that although the moderates knew—or believed they knew—the general framework of Solon's constitution, they 'did not consider self-evident the possibility of getting back to the time before Kleisthenes by research among documents'.[42]

13

Whichever explanation is correct, it seems to be clear that the group responsible for Kleitophon's Rider claimed Solon as their model, and regarded his constitution as basically non-democratic. This is attested by the fourth-century conservative tradition of Solon, the tracing of which *may serve to place the Solon clause in its wider setting*, especially if this trend is seen against the two other tendencies, the democratic and the oligarchic respectively. The references to Solon before 411 are few, especially in a political context. There is practically no mention of his political activities in Herodotos, and his name does not occur at all in Thukydides. In Aristoph. *Nubes* it is said Σόλων ὁ παλαιὸς ἦν φιλόδημος (v. 1187). It might perhaps be taken as an indication that Solon was regarded as a philo-democratic statesman, but this is rather slight evidence. He occurs some years later in Eupolis' *Demoi* as one of the four Athenian worthies conjured up from the dead to find a remedy for Athens' evil plight (Eupolis, Fr. 9, *Demia-ñczuk, Suppl. Comicum*)[43] but no specially important rôle seems to have been attributed to him, and there is no specific mention, in the preserved fragments, of his politics. The motivation of Kleitophon's Rider seems to be the earliest evidence for the use of the name of Solon in party politics. It seems to show that some time before 411 the moderates developed a view of Solon's constitution as a basically non-democratic 'ancestral constitution' to be striven for.

After the democratic restoration of 403 (see below,

14

pp. 33 sqq.), and throughout most of the fourth century, the references to Solon become very frequent, and the fourth-century orators are never tired of singing his praises.[44] Most of the references cited have little to do with politics. But, though Solon's reforms are hardly mentioned by the fourth-century orators, the scope of their remarks sometimes widens. Solon appears, for instance, as 'benevolent towards you and democratic', 'the most democratic', 'the statesman who adorned the Athenian democracy with most beautiful laws', 'the lawgiver who established democracy'.[45] A picture is being evolved and impressed on the mind of the Athenian public of Solon the paragon of all democratic virtue, the democratic lawgiver to whom the law-courts owe their status and the people in general their power—Solon the founder of the democratic state. And this popular view is often echoed in later tradition.[46] This 'democratization of Solon' went further than oratorical eulogy. Solon's work seems to have been discussed in the fourth century and democratically interpreted. At the same time the interest of the moderates in Solon continued and we have indications of their interpretation of Solon's work; and there are some traces of a third, oligarchical, tendency at work.

In the account of Solon's seisachtheia given in Plut. *Sol.* 15 a different view of Androtion is quoted as follows: 'Some people . . . and Androtion is one of them, affirm that the poor were relieved not by a cancelling of debts (χρεῶν ἀποκοπή), but by reduction of the interest upon them, and showed their satisfaction by giving the name of seisachtheia to this act of humanity, and to the augmentation of measures and the change in the purchasing power of money which accompanied it' (*F.Gr.H.* 324, F. 34). Androtion is named here as one of a number of people who hold the seisachtheia to have been not a general cancellation of debts but a measure of poor relief coupled with alterations in the weights and measures. Androtion's main point is then that the seisachtheia was not a great revolutionary measure, but a relatively harmless economic device. This view is explicitly rejected by Plutarch (*ibid.* 15,5–6, cf. *Comp. Sol.-Poplic.* 3,1–2). Aristotle does not expressly mention Androtion's opinion in the *Ath. Pol.* But Solon's measure is repeatedly referred to as a χρεῶν ἀποκοπή (*Ath. Pol.* 6,1; 10,1; 11,2; 12,4) and in ch. 10 the alterations in weights and measures are said to have taken place after (μετά) and not as Androtion contends concurrently (ἅμα) with the cancellation of debts. Details of the alterations, differing from those given by Androtion, follow.[47] Since he certainly knew Androtion's *Atthis* Aristotle's account of the seisachtheia looks very much like an implicit dispute with Androtion.[48] The view concerning the seisachtheia adhered to in the *Ath. Pol.* and in Plut. *Sol.*[49] is widely accepted by modern scholars, and seems to be the correct account of Solon's social measures. Nevertheless, it probably reflects the democratic tradition of Solon. The term seisachtheia does not occur in the preserved verses of Solon; nor was it to be found in Solon's

16

poems known to Aristotle, or he would not say that 'people call these measures seisachtheia' (*Ath. Pol.* 6,1). And, in Androtion's view, it was thus called *by the poor* who benefited from it.⁵⁰ Both the name and the view seem to embody a democratic tradition of Solon's work, though its exact date cannot be ascertained. Whether Androtion took issue with the democratic interpretation or propounded his own view of Solon independently we cannot tell with certainty. At any rate, the tendency to minimize the revolutionary, pro-democratic, character of the seisachtheia would seem to fit in well with the views of Kleitophon and those who considered Kleisthenes' constitution as 'not democratic, but closely akin to that of Solon'.

The democratic and the oligarchic traditions about Solon are to be found in a clash in the alleged sequel to the seisachtheia, the story of the Chreokopidai. Before introducing his main social measure Solon told of his plans— so runs the story in *Ath. Pol.* 6,2–4—to some of his aristocratic friends. They borrowed large sums of money, bought great estates, and became very rich after the cancellation of debts. They were afterwards called 'those of ancient wealth'. That is the story of those who attempt to traduce Solon (πειρῶνταί τινὲς διαβάλλειν αὐτόν). These slanderers (βουλόμενοι βλασφημεῖν) maintained that Solon himself was a party to the deception. According to the democratic account Solon's friends abused his confidence, Solon was not a party to the fraud. Aristotle rejects outright the account hostile to Solon in view of Solon's character as revealed both in his actions and his poems, and stresses his adherence to the democratic version (τῶν δημοτικῶν λόγος).[51] In Plut. *Sol.* 15,6–7 the friends are Konon, Kleinias, and Hipponikos (they were afterwards called Chreokopidai); the view hostile to Solon is rejected; a proof of his innocence is produced—it transpired after the seisachtheia that Solon lost 5 (according to another version 15) talents which were due to him; [52] thus Solon's name was cleared. A short version of this story is given in *Moral.* 807D–E—Solon's innocence is again proclaimed.[53] Plutarch's story implies that Solon came to be suspected of complicity in the fraud of his friends, but the specific indictment referred to in *Ath. Pol.* 6,2 is not reproduced. The common ground for Aristotle and Plutarch seems to be the pro-Solonian version only. Aristotle could regard the names as matters of detail not worth mentioning, and disbelieve the story of Solon's financial losses, or prefer to it his own general statement ex Solon. At any rate comparison seems to show that while Plutarch follows the pro-Solonian story, Aristotle handles both that and the version inimical to Solon, and adheres to the first, stating the grounds for his preference; also, that the version favourable to Solon, which implies the anonymous attack on him, arose as an answer to the slanderers. It is scarcely a plausible supposition that these stories arose in Solon's time among those who suffered financial losses through Solon's measure and wanted to vilify him and his friends.[54] The precise figures given for the sums allegedly lost by Solon are rather suspicious, particularly as three different accounts are given, none of which seems to fit in with the economic conditions of the early sixth century,[55] and especially in view of the fact that Solon was 'in wealth and position . . . of the middle class' (*Ath. Pol.* 5,3). Furthermore, the ὅθεν φασὶ γενέσθαι τοὺς ὕστερον δοκοῦντας εἶναι παλαιοπλούτους, which I take to have been included in the anti-Solonian version, would seem to show that this version was later than Solon's time. That both accounts are late inventions is more likely; and there seem to be some indications (especially if we suppose that the attacks on Solon both in *Ath. Pol.* 6,2 and *Ath. Pol.* 9,2 come from the same source) of the late fifth-century and party-political origin of the story. The anti-Solonian version attacks: (*a*) Solon's personal character; (*b*) the deliberate ambiguity of his laws, allegedly designed for the benefit of the demos (9, 2); (*c*) the families to which Alkibiades, Kallias and Konon belonged. All this seems to fit in with the tendencies of Kritias' group.[56] The clearly oligarchic attack on Solon as responsible for the popular courts created, allegedly, in order to give a preponderant influence to the poor (Arist. *Pol.* Bk. II, ch. 12, cf. below, pp. 20 sqq.) is cognate in spirit with that in *Ath. Pol.* 9,2 and it would seem that the views reflected in *Ath. Pol.* 9,2 are those of the *extremists*.[57] Furthermore, Alkibiades was regarded by Kritias and his men as a most dangerous enemy;[58] an attack on his family, with which that of Kallias and Hipponikos was related by marriage, would seem likely on the part of the extremists of this time. Finally, in view of

Pol. II, 12, and *Ath. Pol.* 9,2 an attempt of the oligarchs of 403 to vilify Solon's personal character would not be surprising. It is doubtful whether this was to be found in an Ἀθηναίων πολιτεία by Kritias,[59] especially as an *Ath. Pol.* by Kritias is not attested. But that these views derive from Kritias' group is, I think, a likely supposition. If that is correct the democratic version may be assumed to have arisen some time after the restoration.[60]

In Arist. *Pol.* II, 12, 1273B35–1274A21,[61] two widely divergent views on Solon's work are to be seen, with Aristotle judiciously moderating. The first trend is introduced by: 'Solon is thought by some people (ἔνιοι) to have been a good legislator'; then their reasons are given '(because) he put an end to unlimited oligarchy (ὀλιγαρχίαν καταλῦσαι λίαν ἄκρατον), emancipated the people, established the ancestral democracy (δημοκρατίαν . . . τὴν πάτριον) and harmonized the different elements of the state (μίξαντα . . . καλῶς).' According to the view of those ἔνιοι: 'the Council of the Areiopagos was an oligarchical element, the elected magistracy, aristocratical, and the courts of law, democratical.' Aristotle does not quarrel with the general appreciation of Solon as an excellent lawgiver [62] nor with taking his constitution as a 'mixed' one. He appends, however, a criticism on a matter of fact. It would seem—he contends—that Solon found the Areiopagos already in existence, as well as the system of electing magistrates; he added only the last element. Thus the μίξις developed; it was not due to Solon's deliberate efforts. The question of

20

fact apart, it seems that the anonymous views referred to by Aristotle tally on the whole with some opinions of the Theramenean group, and with later moderate tradition. The ἔνιοι interpreted Solon's as a mixed constitution. That was, as we have seen, one of the main features of the regime envisaged by the moderates, and Kleisthenes and Solon were praised in the later conservative tradition for this very reason.[63] The attitude of the moderates towards extreme oligarchy seems to be close to that indicated in our passage. They were opposed on principle to the 'rule by force' of the oligarchs and to an enslavement of the Athenian demos; [64] they demanded under the rule of the Four Hundred 'to settle the government on a more equal basis', and were opposed to ἄγαν εἰς ὀλίγους ἐλθεῖν.[65] Though Theramenes does not use in his speech, as related in the *Hellenika*, the term ἄκρατος ὀλιγαρχία employed in *Pol.* 1273, his opposition to those 'who think that there cannot be established true oligarchy (καλὴ ὀλιγαρχία), before they have brought the state under the tyranny of few' [66] comes to very much the same thing. And Isokrates' severe criticism of oligarchy,[67] though not uninfluenced by considerations of expediency, is a case in point. The specification of the elements of the μικτὴ πολιτεία is not to be found in other evidence concerning the moderates but some of the elements are attested. Aristotle rejects the view that the Areiopagos was created by Solon, not only here, but also, implicitly, in the *Ath. Pol.* 8,2–4 (esp. ὥσπερ ὑπῆρχεν καὶ πρότερον, cf. also *ibid.* 3,6). The attribution of

21

the Areiopagos to Solon was known also to Plutarch, who discusses it at length in *Vit. Sol.* 19, argues against it, and winds up with a *non liquet*. It is a likely supposition that the view referred to in the *Pol.*, *Ath. Pol.*, and Plut. *Sol.* goes back to the same source, especially since a common atthidographic source was utilized by Aristotle in the *Ath. Pol.*, and by one of Plutarch's authorities in *Vit. Sol.* It has been suggested that it was Androtion who might have been responsible for attributing to Solon the creation of the Areiopagos.[68] Isokrates' belief in the paramount importance of the Areiopagos in the ideal 'ancestral constitution' of Solon [69] would seem to allow the hypothesis that such a view might have originated in Isokrates' school.[70] There is no evidence that this was already the view of the fifth-century moderates, and it would seem safer to take it as a later development. But the restitution of the powers of the Areiopagos seems to have been included in the moderate platform, as one of the first measures taken by the Thirty in the first, moderate, stage of their rule (cf. below, pp. 76 sqq.) was the abolition of the laws of Ephialtes and Archestratos concerning the Areiopagos.[71] With regard to the element of αἵρεσις referred to by Aristotle, one may recall that to Isokrates a αἵρεσις ἐκ προκρίτων was a feature of the Solonian constitution, and a guarantee of competent, aristocratic, leadership.[72] The method adopted in the first stage of the rule of the Thirty mentioned above is indicated in: 'after appointing a Council of Five Hundred and other magistrates out of a thousand selected candidates (ἐκ προκρίτων)', *Ath. Pol.* 35,1; and that is envisaged also in the advance plan of the moderates (*Ath. Pol.* 30); while election by lot is restricted to the lower offices.[73] Concerning the last element, the law-courts: these are not dealt with in the advance plan of the moderates, while the evidence of *Ath. Pol.* 35,2 (τὸ κῦρος ὃ ἦν ἐν τοῖς δικασταῖς κατέλυσαν) is negative, as it does not supply any information on the organization of the law-courts adopted.[74] The most likely hypothesis is, in my opinion, that of Ferguson who maintains that in the moderate regime of 411–10 'the old Heliastic system continued to exist, the essential reform here consisting of the abolition of pay and the exclusion from service of all citizens who were incapable of equipping themselves with arms and armour. The *nomothetae* may have made alterations in the old method of drawing dikasts and impanelling them for service . . . its members were taken from the three Councils inactive at the moment.'[75]

The second set of views referred to by Aristotle in 1273B–1274A is that of the critics of Solon (μέμφονταί τινες αὐτῷ). They made Solon responsible for the extreme democracy and for complete destruction of the non-democratic elements in Athens' constitution through the creation of the popular law-courts. That seems to be in the same strain as the views of the critics of Solon who maintained that he deliberately drew up his laws with lack of clearness and much scope for dispute in order to give decisive power in the state to the democratic law-courts.[76] In fact, the views rejected by Aristotle in the *Ath. Pol.*, which we have attempted to trace back to the group around Kritias, look very much like *a sequel* to those related in *Pol.* 1273B–1274A. Aristotle rejects the oligarchic criticism of Solon in the *Politics* as he does in the *Ath. Pol.* According to him the critics blamed Solon for unintended and unforeseen consequences of his measures. The later developments would not have resulted from Solon's institution of the law-courts, if it had not been for accidental circumstances, i.e. the naval victories of the Persian wars which gave real power to the demos. Solon was far from intending to found an extreme democracy; he gave only a modicum of power to the people, without which the demos would have been in a state of slavery, and consequently inimical to any government.

The last evidence for resorting to the name of Solon in party-political controversy is of 322 B.C. The revival of the 'ancestral constitution' of Solon was then again mooted by the political group responsible for the change of constitution effected under Antipatros' auspices. Phokion is reported in Plut. *Phoc.* 7,5 to have been desirous 'to restore and carry out the polity, more complete in itself (ὁλόκληρον) and more harmonious and uniform, which prevailed in the times of Perikles, Aristeides, and Solon'. Thus the condition imposed by Antipatros on the Athenians: πολιτευο-μένοις . . . τὴν πάτριον ἀπὸ τιμήματος πολιτείαν . . . Plut. *Phoc.* 27,5, was at least highly acceptable to Phokion's group, if not actually suggested by them and endorsed by

Antipatros. It would seem to be clear in view of the passages quoted above, and Diodoros' κατὰ τοὺς Σόλωνος νόμους ἐπολιτεύοντο,[77] that the rule of the propertied classes (ἀπὸ τιμήσεως πολίτευμα ... Diod. 18, 18,4), with the exclusion of those with incomes less than two thousand drachmai, was established under the slogan of 'return to Solon's ancestral constitution'.[78]

The conservative tradition, which has its roots in the political ideas of the Theramenean group, helps to some degree to evaluate the attitude of late fifth-century moderates towards Solon and Kleisthenes. Taken in conjunction with the views of the fifth-century moderates it contributes, I submit, to the understanding of Kleitophon's Rider.

NOTES TO CHAPTER I

1. Cf. Swoboda, *Griech. Volksbeschlüsse* (1890), pp. 13 sqq.; Hartel, *Stud. üb. Att. Staatsrecht* (1878), pp. 221 sqq.
2. I am told by Professor Wade-Gery that he has discarded since the latter supposition.
3. Cf. also below, pp. 63 sqq.
4. For further evidence on Kleitophon and discussion, cf. Wade-Gery, *op. cit.*, p. 20; for the historical context, and for Kleitophon's amendment as a motion of the moderates proposed after the acceptance of the decree of the extremist Pythodoros, cf. especially Wilcken, *Sitzb. Preuss. Ak.*, 1935, p. 38; Jacoby, *op. cit.*, p. 384, n. 30; Kunle, *Unters. üb. d. achte Buch d. Thuk.* (1909), p. 45; Busolt-(Swoboda), *Staatskunde*, I, p. 70; see also Ballet, *Mus. Belge* 2 (1898), p. 7; Dümler, *Hermes* 27 (1892), p. 263. On the Rider see also Sartori, *La Crisi del 411 A.C.* (1951), pp. 25 sqq.; van der Ploeg, *Theramenes en zijn Tijd* (1948), p. 21.
5. Cf. 5,69,2 and 5,66,2 (see also on Kleisthenes 5,67; 5,70,2; 5,72,1; 5,73,1).

6. Larsen, 'Cleisthenes and the development of the theory of democracy', *Essays in political theory presented to Sabine* (1948), pp. 4, 13 sqq.

7. Thuc. 8,53,1.

8. Thuc. 8,51,3–8,54,2; cf. Thuc. 8,86,3.

9. If Ps.-Xen. *A.II.* is, as I believe, a polemic against the views of the moderates (cf. Ed. Meyer, *Forsch.* 2, pp. 401 sqq.; Müller-Strübing, *Philol. Supplement.* 4 (1884)) the ὥστε μέντοι ὑπάρχειν μὲν δημοκρατίαν εἶναι in *A.II.* 3,9 could be taken as an evidence that the moderates had no quarrel on principle with the term *demokratia.* (Cf. also *Hell.* 2,3,48–9, where Theramenes rejects the extreme democracy, not, it seems, democracy as such.)

10. On Isokrates' political views cf. especially: Jaeger, *Harv. St. Cl. Phil.*, Suppl. 1 (1940), pp. 428 sq., 430, 440, 441 sqq. (cf. *idem, Paidcia* 3, 1945, pp. 106 sqq.); Mathieu, *Les idées politiq. d'Isocrate* (1925), pp. 126 sqq.; Pöhlmann, 'Isokrates und das Problem der Demokratie', *Sitzb. Münch. Ak.*, 1913; Keil, *Die Solon. Verfass. in Arist. Verfassungsgesch. Athens* (1892), pp. 78 sqq.; Wilamowitz, *Ar. u. Ath.* 2, pp. 380 sqq., cf. 1, p. 167; cf. Larsen, *op. cit.*, p. 16; see also below, note 21. [Cloché's article in *Ét. Class.* 5 (1936), pp. 394 sqq., was inaccessible to me.]

11. Cf. Isocr. 8, 38, 75, 80–8, 108, 121–3 (see also Koch, *Quo modo Isocrates saec. 5 res ennarraverit*, 1914, pp. 48 sqq.).

12. Main evidence: 4, 76–7; 5, 129; 7, 13–16, 20, 24, 50–3, 56–9, 62, 72 sq., 76, 77 sq., 79 sqq.; 8, 4, 12–14, 36, 38–56, 75–7, 82–8, 115, 119, 121–31; 12, 15 sq., 118, 131, 133, 139–42; 15, 18 sq., 22, 126, 138, 142, 154, 291 sqq., 301, 303, 398, 312, 314, ʼ317, sq., 320; cf. Pöhlmann, *op cit.*; see also note 21.

13. 7, 16, cf. 59; 15, 231–5, 306; 16, 26–7.

14. Cf. 7,16,60–1 (καλῶς καθεστηκυῖα δημοκρατία), cf. 70; 12,147; 15,232; 16,26; 8,64.—Although Isokrates does not employ the term πάτριος δημοκρατία his 'ancient democracy' seems to be close to the 'ancestral democracy' praised by the people who approve of Solon's 'ancestral democracy' but are opposed to the later ἄκρατος δημοκρατία. Cf. Arist. *Pol.* 1273, B, 35 sqq., and on this passage, see pp. 20 sqq.

15. Cf. evidence quoted in note 12.—(It may be worth noting that the δημοκρατίαν κατέστησε is always coupled in Isokrates with τυράννους ἐκβαλών. The fact that Kleisthenes had established a *constitutional* form of government may perhaps explain some of the appeal he had both for Isokrates and for the constitutionalist moderate group of the late fifth century.)

26

16. See also Larsen, *op. cit.*, p. 15.

17. Aristotle has permitted himself also otherwise some liberty in relating the Rider; ἔγραψε is Aristotle's addition, <ἄν> an omission (cf. Kaibel, *Stil u. Text d. Ath. Pol.*, 1893, p. 187).

18. The opening sentence of the decree of Patrokleides is a well-known instance; cf. also (e.g.) Tod, *Gr. Hist. Inscr.*[2] nos. 89,4 sqq.; 91,30 sq.; 131,35 sqq.; 178,5 sqq.

19. Aristotle records the name of Melobios, who made the speech before the psephisma of Pythodoros (*Ath. Pol.* 29,1); the Rider was probably also preceded by such a speech (for a λόγος before the motion cf. also e.g. Lys. 12,73).

20. Cf. 21; 20,1; 20,4; 41,2; *Pol.* 1275B, 34–8, 1319B, 1 sqq.; τὰ δημοτικώτατα of Solon (*Ath. Pol.* 9. 1) 'do not refer to a democratic constitution, or to constitution at all. They were to indicate certain foundations on which democracy was to be built' (Ehrenberg, *Historia* I (1950), p. 538).

21. Main evidence: 4, 54, 68, 77; 7, 15–30, 41–2, 44, 47, 51, 56–61, 72 sq., 76, 78 sqq.; 8, 64, 75 sq., 90, 93 sq., 133–5; 12, 54, 130 sqq., 145, 146, 148, 153, 197, 312; 15, 231–5, 306, 313 ;16, 26–7. On Isokrates' 'ancestral constitution' see especially Jaeger, *op. cit.*, pp. 441 sqq., cf. *Paideia*, 3, pp. 114 sqq.; Jacoby, *op. cit.*, 75; Pöhlmann, *op. cit.*, pp. 110 sqq.; Mathieu, *op. cit.*, pp. 140 sqq.; *id. Rev. Phil.* 38 (1914), p. 188 sq.; Hirzel, Ἄγραφος νόμος, *Abh. Sächs. Ak.* 20 (1900), pp. 75 sqq.; Jost, *Das Beispiel und Vorbild der Vorfahren* (1936), pp. 140 sqq.; Larsen, *op. cit.*, p. 15; Dümler, *Hermes* 27 (1892), pp. 274 sqq.; also Schmitz-Kahlmann, *Beispiel d. Gesch. im polit. Denken d. Isokr.* (1939), pp. 101 sqq.; Bock, *Würzb. Jahrb.* 4 (1949–50), pp. 226 sqq.

22. 7,16; 15,231–5,306; 16,26–7.

23. It may be worth noting that the Athenian constitution previous to the Persian wars, i.e. basically the Kleisthenean, is, implicitly, praised by as 'conservative' a writer as Plato; cf. *Leg.* 698B.—(The meaning and the origin of the saying: ἀπόλοιντο οἱ Κλεισθένεις καὶ οἱ Δράκοντες Alciphr. Fr. 2, cf. [Plato], *Axioch.* 365d is obscure—notwithstanding the comment of Ziehen, *Rh. Mus.* 54, 1899, p. 334).

24. Xen. *Hell.* 2,3,48–9; Thuc. 8,97,2; Arist. *Pol.*, especially 1296A, 36–40 (cf. also Eurip. Fr. 21; *Suppl.* 238–45.)

25. 12, 153 and 131; cf. also p. 10 (see also Zillig, *Die Theorie von d. Gemischten Verfass.*, 1916, pp. 20 sqq.).—For the topicality of the slogans

27

of ὁμόνοια and σωτηρία in late fifth-century politics, from which Plutarch's source may originally derive, cf. p. 12 sq.; cf. pp. 103 sq., 106, n. 6; and Thuc. 8,72,1–2; 8,86,3; 8,53,2; Ath. Pol. 29,2–3; see also Bieler, A.J.Ph. 72 (1951), pp. 181 sqq.

26. Cf. Diod. 11,77,6; see also Johnson, A.J.Ph. 58 (1937), p. 334.

27. The correct historical context is after Kimon's return from Ithome. (That seems to have been made out by Ed. Meyer, Forsch. 2, pp. 50 sqq. Cf. G.d.A. 4³, pp. 535 sqq.)

28. Main evidence: 7, 21–8, 37, 61; 8, 133; 12, 130 sqq., 143–8, 153–4; 15, 132, 308 (cf. 3,14); see also note 21; cf. Jaeger, pp. 113, 152.—For the term καλοὶ κἀγαθοί in connection with the moderate movement, see (f. i.): Xen. Hell. 2,3,15; 19; 49; 53; Ath. Pol., Epit. Heracl. 7; Plut. Pericl. 11,2; Ath. Pol. 28,5; Aristoph. Ran. 717 sqq.; cf. also Ath. Pol. 36,1–2 (ἐπιεικεῖς); (for fuller general evidence Berlage, De vi et usu vocum καλὸς κἀγαθός, καλοκἀγαθία, Mnemosyne 60, 1932, pp. 20 sqq.).

29. 7,57 sqq., cf. 3 sqq. and 70; cf. 8,39.

30. Cf. evidence quoted in note 21 and especially 7,27; 58 sq.; 12,120 sq., 147,151.

31. Cf. especially Ath. Pol. 36,2; 28,5; Hell. 2,3,19; 2,3,45; 2,3,48–9; Lys. 34,1.

32. Ath. Pol. 35,2; cf. Isocr. 8,133; Ps.-Xen. A.Π. 3,8–9; see also p. 4 sq. and n. 9.

33. Cf. e.g. Pol. 1296A, 1 sqq., especially 36–40; also 1297B, 1 sqq.

34. See Goodhart, The 8th Bk. of Thuc. (1893), ad loc.; cf. Classen, ad loc.

35. Cf. e.g. Meyer, Forsch. 2, p. 403.

36. ἀριστοκρατία σώφρων in Thuc. 3,82,8 may, perhaps, be an allusion to a name the moderate groups in Greek politics wanted to be called by.

37. According to Dem. 23,205 it is Kimon, not the democrats, who τὴν πάτριον (not Παρίων) μετεκίνησε πολιτείαν ἐφ' ἑαυτοῦ. In his story (l.c.) Kimon's trial consequent on his Macedonian campaign, his ostracism, his action in connection with the Areiopagos, and also the trial of Miltiades seem to be all confused (cf. Meyer, Forsch. 2, p. 25 n.); in addition the passage implies that his attempt to restore the powers of the Areiopagos was successful. That embodies the opposed, democratic, tradition of the events; π.π. stands here for democracy; cf. below, pp. 33 sqq.

38. See Jacoby, Atthis, pp. 75 sqq., 106, 114, 123, 154 sq., 160, 212, 214,

28

317 sq., 383; cf. also Pearson, *Local Historians of Attica* (1942), pp. 14, 39, 67, 82, 111, 118, 159.

39. *Forsch.* 2, especially pp. 50 sqq.; the exceptions taken by Uxkull-Gyllenband, *Plut. und d. Griech. Biographie* (1927), p. 73, carry, in my opinion, little weight.

40. Jacoby, *op. cit.*, p. 79: 'The majority of the authors of *Atthides* belonged to the conservative party: Androtion, Phanodemos, and Philochoros were more or less "reactionaries". As to Melanthios and Demon ... we may believe them to have been the same. But they were conservatives, not right-wing extremists ...'; cf. also Bloch, *Harv. St. Cl. Phil.*, Suppl. 1, p. 352.

41. Cf. above nn. 15 and 21.

42. Jacoby, *op. cit.*, p. 206; he continues: 'indeed ... records of the Council from the time of Solon did not exist. .... It is not credible that records, in the proper sense of the word, should have existed in the sixth century at all'. If this is correct it seems to follow that whatever their propagandist reasons the moderates had in mind a search among the documents and reckoned, when formulating the Rider, with its practical possibilities. Cf. also op. cit., p. 215.

43. Cf. Edmonds, *Mnemos.* 3, ser. 8 (1939–40), p. 5.

44. Main evidence: Aesch. 1, 6–7, 25–6, 183; 3, 38, 108, 175, 257; Demosth. 18, 6–7; 19, 251–6; 20, 90–93; 102–4; 22, 25, 30–32; 24, 103, 113, 142, 138, 211–12; [26], 4, 23; [42], 1; [43], 62, 66–7, 78; [44], 67–8; [46], 14; [48], 56; 57, 31; [61], 49–50; Hyper. 3, 21–2; Isaeus, 2, 13 (cf. 3,42; see Wyse, *Speeches of Isaeus* (1904), p. 325); Lyc. *Leocr.* 64; Lys. 10, 15; 30, 2, 18, 26, 28.

45. Demosth. 18,6–7; Hyp. 3,21–2; Aesch. 3,257 and 3,38; (cf. Lys. 30,28); see also Pearson, *C.P.* 36 (1941), pp. 221 sqq.

46. Cf. e.g.: Plut. *Sol.* 16,2; *Comp. Sol. Poplic.* 2,1; *Mor.* 152A, C; Diog. Laert. *Vit. Sol. pass.* (cf. also Philem., Fr. 4, Kock).

47. Plut. *Sol.* 15,4; *Ath. Pol.* 10,2 (cf., however, Reinach's conjecture in *Hermes* 63, 1928, pp. 238–40).

48. Cf. Keil, *Solon. Verf.*, p. 45 sq.; Adcock, *Klio* 12 (1912), p. 5; Jacoby, *op. cit.*, p. 213.

49. Cf. also e.g. Diod. 1,79,4; Diog. Laert. *Sol.* 45; Plut. *Mor.* 807E; Suid. *s.v.* (the side taken by Philochoros, quoted there = *F. Gr. Hist.* 328, F. 114, is not clear enough).

29

50. Cf. Linforth, *Solon the Athenian* (1919), pp. 269 sqq.; cf. also the evidence in Gilliard, *Réform. de Solon* (1907), p. 191.

51. In 9,2 he rejects again the views of those who want to incriminate Solon, most probably those responsible for the story of the Chreokopidai. Their incriminations were that 'Solon deliberately made the laws indefinite in order that the final decision might be in the hands of the people'; cf. 35,2 and p. 23 sq.

52. The latter figure was given by Polyzelos, cf. *F. Gr. Hist.* 521, F. 8; Diog. Laert. *Sol.* 45 refers to seven talents due to Solon when the seisachtheia came into force.

53. A variant of a version hostile to Solon, based, it seems, on misunderstanding, is given in Suid. *s.v. Σόλων.*

54. That is the view taken, e.g., by Freeman, *The Work and Life of Solon* (1926), p. 87 sq.

55. Adcock, *op. cit.*, p. 10.

56. Cf. Dümmler, *Hermes* 27 (1892), pp. 260 sqq.

57. Those of the Laws of Solon which were ambiguously worded were repealed by the Thirty (*Ath. Pol.* 35,2). Although the moderates would probably have wished for such an improvement, it can hardly be supposed in view of their general attitude towards Solon that they could have imputed to him the rather sinister reasons mentioned in *Ath. Pol.* 9,2.

58. Cf. Armbruster, *Über d. Herrschaft d. Dreissig* (1913), pp. 48 sqq.

59. Dümmler, *op. cit.*

60. Jacoby, *op. cit.*, p. 75 and n. 25 (p. 294), suggests, tentatively, that the democratic version was to be found in Kleidemos' *Atthis*; the immediate source of Plutarch's story was, according to a conjecture of Prinz, *De Solonis Plutarchei fontibus* (1867)—worked up by Begemann, *Quest. Solon.* (1875)—Hermippos; cf. recently Von der Mühll, *Klio* 35 (1942), pp. 89 sqq.—It seems to be almost certain that Aristotle used Androtion's *Atthis*, but the view, adhered to by some scholars, that in handling the pro-Solonian and the anti-Solonian versions Aristotle follows here Androtion, is open to doubt. Aristotle rejects Androtion's interpretation of the seisachtheia (above, p. 16); probably also his account of Solon's monetary reforms (*ibid.*), and his views concerning the creation of the Areiopagos by Solon (p. 22). In view of this it would seem better to think that in his account of the story of the Chreokopidai Aristotle might have independently handled his evidence (the oligarchic version, the democratic version and,

his most important source, Solon's poems) than to suppose that he rather slavishly follows here Androtion. Whatever was the intrinsic value of Androtion's *Atthis*, and the extent of its utilization by Aristotle, it does not seem to be justifiable to ignore altogether Aristotle's own judgement.

61. There are no sufficient grounds for regarding this passage as an interpolation; so already Wilamowitz, *Ar. u. Ath.* 1, pp. 64 sqq.

62. That was in fact his own view; *Ath. Pol.* 11,2: τὰ βέλτιστα νομοθετήσας, cf. *Pol.* 1296A, 19; *Rhet.* 1398B, 15–20.

63. See above, pp. 8 sqq.; cf. also *Pol.* 1265B, 34 sqq., which may well be the theoretical basis propounded by those whose views are quoted in our passage; cf. Newman, *Politics of Aristotle,* 2 (1887), p. 266 sq.

64. Cf. *Ath. Pol.* 36,2; *Hell.* 2,3,19; Ps.-Xen. *A.II.* 1,9 (see also *C.P.* 39, 1944, p. 143).

65. Thuc. 8,89,2.

66. 2,3,48.

67. Cf. Jaeger, *Paideia* 3, p. 123 sq.; Dümmler, *Hermes* 27 (1892), pp. 269 sqq.

68. Recently, Jacoby, *op. cit.,* p. 74; cf. Keil, p. 193.

69. Cf. especially 7,37 sqq.; 12,154; see Jaeger, *Harv. St. Cl. Phil.,* Suppl. 1, pp. 409 sqq.; Verdam, *De senatu Areopagitico* (1902), pp. 86 sqq.

70. Cf. Keil, *op. cit.,* p. 100 sq.—(For the glorification of the Areiopagos see also, e.g., the well-known ch. 5 of *Memor. Bk.* 3.)

71. *Ath. Pol.* 35,2 (cf. 25,1); see Verdam, *op. cit.,* p. 84; Jaeger, *op. cit.,* pp. 443 sqq.; Busolt-(Swoboda), *Staatsk.,* p. 57; Mathieu, *Rev. Phil.* 38 (1914), p. 188 sq.; Kahrstedt, *Klio* 30 (1937), p. 28; Bury, *C.R.* 9 (1895), p. 108.

72. Cf. for a detailed discussion of Isokrates' views on this point, and for elucidation of Aristotle's own opinions, Keil, *op. cit.,* pp. 77 sqq.; see above, n. 28.

73. Cf. Ehrenberg, *P.W. s.v. Losung,* col. 1468 sqq.; see also Jaeger, *op. cit.,* p. 444.

74. In practice extensive juridical power was usurped by the Thirty in the latter stage of their rule when the extremists seized control of the state.

75. Ferguson, *Mél. Glotz.* 1 (1932), p. 358; cf. his argument *ibid.,* pp. 357 sqq.

76. *Ath. Pol.* 9,2; cf. above, p. 19 and n. 51.

77. 18,18, par. 5; it would seem to stand in this context for Solon's constitution, not for his laws; cf. also Busolt-Swoboda, p. 927.

31

78. That might have been the case also with regard to the rule of Demetrios of Phaleron, when the census was lowered to one thousand drachmai, but not abolished.—On the constitutions established under Phokion, and that of Demetrios respectively, cf. especially Ferguson, *Hellenistic Athens* (1911), pp. 19 sqq.; Busolt-Swoboda, pp. 926 sqq.; Sundwall, *Act. Soc. Sc. Fenn.* 34 (1906), pp. 8 sqq.; Bayer, *Demetrios Phalereus* (1942), pp. 6 sqq.; Dow and Travis, *Hesperia* 12 (1943), pp. 144 sqq.; see also Oncken, *Arist. Staatslehre*, 2 (1875), p. 442.

Chapter II

THE DEMOCRATS
AND *ΠΑΤΡΙΟΣ ΠΟΛΙΤΕΙΑ*

IN chapters 74-7 of book VIII Thukydides narrates the events which put an end to the oligarchic movement in Samos; in 76,3 sqq. he records some of the arguments put forward in the Assembly in which the strategoi suspected of oligarchic inclinations were deposed and democratic influence well established under Thrasybulos and Thrasyllos. One of the arguments propounded by the democrats (par. 6) was τοὺς μὲν (i.e. the anti-democratic opposition at Athens) ἡμαρτηκέναι τοὺς πατρίους νόμους καταλύσαντας, αὐτοὶ δὲ σῴζειν καὶ ἐκείνους πειράσεσθαι προσαναγκάζειν (i.e. σῴζειν τοὺς πατρίους νόμους). Νόμοι means in this context πολιτεία; the term 'ancestral laws' stands here for democracy. It is the democratic regime abolished some weeks previously at the Kolonos under the slogan of a return to the 'ancestral constitution' which is to the democrats the true πάτριος πολιτεία to be striven for. Speaking of the restoration of 'ancestral laws' the democrats seem to look back some weeks, rather than some generations.

According to Xenophon's account of the first meeting

of the Assembly after the return of the democratic exiles in 403, Thrasybulos wound up his speech with the exhortation to create no confusion, but live according to the ancient laws (τοῖς νόμοις τοῖς ἀρχαίοις χρῆσθαι) (*Hell.* 2,4,42). Ἀρχαῖοι νόμοι is used here, I suggest, in the sense in which πάτριοι νόμοι was used in the democratic Assembly in Samos, in which Thrasybulos was the most prominent figure.[1] The supposition that to Thrasybulos democracy as it stood before the rule of the Thirty was the 'ancient laws' to be restored seems to be in accord with the events which followed the first Assembly, and with the opening clauses of the Decree of Teisamenos. This decree (Andoc. I, 83–4) is introduced and explained by Andokides in paragraphs 81–2, where he succeeds in obscuring the antecedents and the purpose of the document. His explanations call for some comment before we turn to the decree itself. After the return of the exiles and the proclamation of amnesty a Committee of Twenty was chosen to take care of the city ἕως [ἂν] οἱ νόμοι τεθεῖεν . . . (par. 81). It would seem certain that they had to 'take care of the city' in general, but ἕως οἱ νόμοι τεθεῖεν, if it denotes time-limit, does not seem to be probable. It would seem to mean here (as it means in Pseph.-Teis.) 'completion of the laws'.[2] That had been brought about by 401 (cf. below, p. 38), but there is no clear indication that the Twenty played any part in the nomothetic process; in fact there is no room for them in the elaborate scheme envisaged in the decree of Teisamenos (below, p. 36 sq.). Nor do they appear in any other capacity

34

after the date of Pseph.-Teis., though we have evidence for their activity before its date. The council of the Five Hundred was constituted before Teisamenos' proposal (Andoc. I, 81); also two nomothetic bodies were elected (see below, p. 36), and the normal *archai* were already acting by the time of Teisamenos' proposal. The Twenty gave place, I think, to the normal democratic organs they had re-established, and to the nomothetic bodies, which were to take care of such legislation as was needed. If we judge by the effects of their activities, we shall have to conclude that the re-establishment of the normal democratic organs—and the setting up of the special nomothetic bodies required for new legislation—were the only tasks imposed on the Twenty in their mandate. According to Andokides' next statement, the laws of Solon and the thesmoi of Drakon were to be *provisionally* in force. That appears to be false on comparison with the decree of Teisamenos, which deals in greater detail with this matter. The nomoi of Solon and Drakon's thesmoi are conceived in Pseph.-Teis. as the fundamental permanent Law of Athens (for details, see below, pp. 38 sqq.). Andokides continues 'and when you chose the council and elected the nomothetai they kept finding that according to many of the laws of Solon and Drakon many citizens were inculpated because of previous events. You called meetings of Assembly and decreed on a dokimasia of all the laws, etc.' That is suspect on more than one point. A dokimasia of the entire body of laws is not borne out by the decree of Teisamenos, which speaks

35

of additional legislation only (though it possibly led to revision of some of the older laws). As regards the reasons for the legislation to be undertaken, they are couched by Andokides in terms which seem to serve his own ends.[3] However, the general purpose of the legislation envisaged in Pseph.-Teis. seems to have been the supplementing of the previous codification (cf. below, pp. 37 sqq.) by legislation called for by the rule of the Thirty and the subsequent amnesty.[4] By and large, interpretation of the decree of Teisamenos in the light of Andokides' partly tendentious, partly muddled explanations seems to be a wrong course, and to lead nowhere.[5] The decree of Teisamenos itself is our only reliable source and Andokides' statements could be valid only in so far as they are borne out by the document.

The opening clause of the decree says: (a) πολιτεύεσθαι Ἀθηναίους κατὰ τὰ πάτρια. According to the next clause (b) the laws valid are to be those of Solon with the thesmoi of Drakon (which were included in the laws of Solon); (c) these are the laws (and weights and measures): οἷσπερ ἐχρώμεθα ἐν τῷ πρόσθεν χρόνῳ; (d) additional laws needed (ὁπόσων δ' ἂν προσδέῃ) are to be drafted by the nomothetai elected by the Council.[6] The laws are to be presented to the magistrates within a month; (e) they are to be examined by the Council together with 500 nomothetai elected by the municipalities; (f) any citizen may give advice to the Council on the laws; (g) after their final ratification the laws are to be published 'on the Wall where the inscription was made before'; (h) the Council of the Areiopagos is enjoined to take care that the laws should be duly observed by the magistrates. The decree of Teisamenos seems to be the first known official document after the restoration of democracy. The normal democratic organs are already active by the time of the decree, and in addition to them there are the two commissions of nomothetai. The Five Hundred were elected by the demotai either before or after the Council was reconstituted.[7] The other board of nomothetai, elected after the reconstitution of the Council, are to be regarded as experts, who, acting as anagrapheis, are to assist the Board of Five Hundred and the Council.[8] The decree provides for supplementation of the laws of Solon and Drakon to meet the needs of 403. The supplementary legislation is to be effected within a month. (The work of legislation is known to have lasted much longer, see below, p. 38. Thus, either their mandate was subsequently extended, or perhaps the expression 'within this month' meant originally that the submitting of the new laws to the Council and the Five Hundred nomothetai was to start within a month.) The decree does not deal with full re-codification of the Athenian law. The work of codification was started after the first democratic restoration, in 410–9, and it continued for about six years, up to the rule of the Thirty. Teisamenos' decree would seem to show that this work was regarded as having been in the main completed, and this seems to be strengthened by the final clause of the decree which envisages publication of the laws

37

on the Wall where the inscription was made before (ἵνα περ πρότερον ἀνεγράφησαν). This clause appears in a new light after the American excavations in the agora in which the inscribed wall spoken of in Pseph.-Teis. was uncovered.⁹ The inscriptions on it are fragments of the Athenian Code of Laws. Those in Ionian script belong to the additional legislation consequent on the decree of Teisamenos, the inscriptions written in the old Attic script are fragments of the laws codified before the archonship of Eukleides. Apparently the lawgivers of 403 could base themselves on work done by their predecessors.¹⁰ The supplementary legislation envisaged in the decree of Teisamenos seems to have been completed by 401.¹¹ Some laws quoted by Andokides, and the law of Diokles, are a sequel, and, as it were, a rounding off of it. The first is: ἀγράφῳ δὲ νόμῳ τὰς ἀρχὰς μὴ χρῆσθαι κτλ. (Andoc. I, 85); ¹² that is expanded in the law quoted in par. 87 (ψήφισμα δὲ μηδὲν . . . νόμου κυριώτερον εἶναι κτλ.). The last states: τοῖς δὲ νόμοις χρῆσθαι ἀπ᾿ Εὐκλείδου ἄρχοντος (Andoc. I, 87).¹³ Finally, the law of Diokles (Dem. 24,42) provides a good summing up.

The opening clauses of the decree of Teisamenos (from ἔδοξε to χρόνῳ)—our main concern here—are to be viewed against this background.

There is a distinction in the decree between πολιτεύεσθαι and νόμοις χρῆσθαι. Athens' constitution is to be κατὰ τὰ πάτρια, whereas the general body of laws in force are to be the nomoi of Solon with the thesmoi (concerning homicide) of Drakon (νόμοις δὲ κτλ.). Evidently only the

38

code of laws was to be Solonian, not the constitution. Hence the view advanced by some modern scholars,[14] that Solon's constitution was to be provisionally re-established, would seem to have no foundation. Nor does the decree of Teisamenos indicate—as is often supposed—an archaistic 'return to Solon and Drakon' in connection with the general body of the Athenian laws. The growth of the nucleus of the Solonian legislation into a body of Athenian law in which the genuine Solonian elements would in very many cases scarcely be recognizable is described, e.g., by Linforth;[15] and Schreiner, *De corpore iuris Atheniensium* (1913), pp. 49 sqq., seems to me to have made out a good case (in spite of some exaggerations) for the supposition that 'Solon's laws' came, already in the fifth century, to mean in general use 'Athenian laws', or 'the body of laws of democratic Athens'.[16] That seems to be the case in the decree of Teisamenos. The use of 'Solonian laws' is not conceived in the psephisma as an innovation. The laws are those 'which we have been using before', i.e., I think, before democracy was abolished by the Thirty and the democratic code tampered with by the oligarchs.[17] It seems to be (as in 410-9, cf. Lys. 30) a restoration of the code of laws of democratic Athens, not a return to the 'genuine laws of Solon' with exclusion of all other Athenian laws which could not be proved to be genuinely Solonian. There remains, however, the question whether πολιτεύεσθαι Ἀθηναίους κατὰ τὰ πάτρια indicates an archaizing tendency, a return to the far-off historical past. The expression κατὰ τὰ πάτρια occurs frequently in various, especially religious, contexts (e.g. θύειν κατὰ τὰ πάτρια); it means an old law or usage and does not in itself supply any clue. However, τὰ πάτρια, πάτριος, πάτριον in connection with πολιτεύεσθαι, πολιτεία and the like are attested several times in the sense of the *existing constitution* or the (historically) *normal* constitution,[18] evidently generally regarded as deriving its authority from the past. The ancestral constitutions warranted in the symmachy between Antigonos and Demetrios on the one side and the Greek cities on the other are the then *existing* constitutions.[19] The restoration of Athens' usual democratic regime after the rules of Phokion and of Demetrios of Phaleron is dubbed 'a reconstitution of the ancestral polity'.[20] It is in this sense, I suggest, that πολιτεύεσθαι κατὰ τὰ πάτρια is used in the decree of Teisamenos; it meant to Teisamenos what πάτριος πολιτεία meant to the democrats of the time of Phokion and Demetrios of Phaleron, πάτριοι νόμοι to the Athenian democrats in Samos, and ἀρχαῖοι νόμοι to Thrasybulos.[21] This seems to be borne out by the use of the term πάτριος πολιτεία in connection with or. 34 of Lysias, contemporary with the decree of Teisamenos.

Towards the end of his essay on Lysias, Dionysios of Halikarnassos quotes as an example of Lysias' deliberative style a speech which ὑπόθεσιν . . . περιείληφε τὴν περὶ τοῦ μὴ καταλῦσαι τὴν πάτριον πολιτείαν Ἀθήνησιν . . . (*de Lys.*, par. 31). A description of the historical circumstances follows. After the return of the democrats (τοῦ δήμου

40

κατελθόντος), Phormisios moved that citizen-rights should be restricted to landowners (τοὺς μὲν φεύγοντας κατιέναι, τὴν δὲ πολιτείαν μὴ πᾶσιν ἀλλὰ τοῖς γῆν ἔχουσι παραδοῦναι). The number of the disfranchised would have been about 5000. It was intimated by Phormisios that Sparta favoured his proposal (par. 32). Lysias' speech was written against this proposal. A long fragment of the speech (or. 34) follows. It opens with an attack on the group with which the proposal originated: 'These men are seeking to deceive us . . . with the selfsame decrees with which they have tricked us twice before' (34,1). To accept this proposal is— according to the speaker—to rob Athens of its power, to reject it is to secure the Athenian democracy (βεβαίως δημοκρατήσεσθε) (par. 4). Many of the propertied class were expelled from the city by the oligarchs (par. 4). They were recalled by the demos who did not dare to appropriate to itself the property of the well-to-do. 'Thus,' the speaker says, addressing himself to the property owners, 'if you take my advice, you will not be depriving your benefactors, so far as you may (καθὸ δύνασθε), of the native land' (par. 5). The remaining paragraphs (6–11) are devoted to the international aspect of Phormisios' proposal. Sparta, who was understood to favour the proposal of Phormisios, will not—Lysias contends—support it by force. If she does, war is better than peace on such terms.

We have, almost certainly, the beginning of the speech, and the final paragraphs look very much like its peroration. Possibly only a small part of the winding up of the speech

41

was omitted by Dionysios.[22] The preserved part verifies on several points Dionysios' introductory remarks. The general trend of pars. 1–5 vouchsafes the correctness of Dionysios' statement that, according to the proposal, citizen-rights were to be given to land-owners.[23] Pars. 6–11 confirm Dionysios' statement that the desirability of the constitutional change to Sparta has been pointed out by Phormisios (de Lys. 32). Phormisios' name does not occur in the preserved part of the speech; it must have been found by Dionysios in Philochoros, or in the part of the speech he fails to quote. The political group to which the proposal fought against by Lysias is ascribed is easily recognizable as the moderates,[24] one of whose leaders was Phormisios.[25]

Dionysios' τοῦ δήμου κατελθόντος ἐκ Πειραιῶς καὶ ψηφισαμένου διαλύσασθαι κτλ. would seem to point to a time shortly after 12 of Boedromion as the date of Phormisios' proposal and of the speech of Lysias. But some other passages both in the speech and in Dionysios' introductory remarks are to be discussed in this connection. According to Dionysios, it was proposed by Phormisios: τοὺς μὲν φεύγοντας κατιέναι, τὴν δὲ πολιτείαν κτλ. (l.c.). The usual explanation is that the exiled democrats are meant here.[26] Cloché,[27] however, points out that there was no need to propose the return of the democratic exiles, since Phormisios' proposal was submitted, whatever be its exact date, after the return of the democrats from Piraeus. He takes the 'refugees' to refer to the oligarchic exiles, who remained outside Athens after

42

the reconciliation, and inclines to date Phormisios' proposal, and with it Lys. or. 34, much later, before the problem of these exiles was finally settled (401). However, the expression φεύγοντας κατελθεῖν is used by Lysias to denote the democratic exiles (par. 2). Furthermore, if the motion of Phormisios had included *two* anti-democratic proposals (i.e. return of the oligarchic exiles, and restriction of franchise), Lysias would have opposed both of them, not only the latter. According to Lenschau [28] the 'refugees' are Athenian kleruchoi who were compelled to leave their domiciles and return to Athens. The limitation of citizen-rights was to apply to them only. However, neither Lysias nor Dionysios seems to be aware of the question of the kleruchoi being dealt with in Phormisios' proposal. There were probably kleruchoi among those shepherded to Athens by Lysandros before the siege in 405; [29] and we do not know of an outstanding problem of the kleruchoi in 403. The language of Dionysios, which gives the impression that a proposal concerning the return of the exiles was included in Phormisios' motion, seems to be somewhat misleading. If the refugees were mentioned in the motion of Phormisios it may have been in some such connection as 'not all of the exiles have to enjoy citizen-rights but only . . . etc.', or 'the citizens banished must for the most part be content with their restoration' [30] or the like. At any rate, φεύγοντας κατιέναι cannot be used as evidence for a late date; if it is to be taken as evidence at all, it would rather agree with a date shortly after 12 of Boedromion.

43

Another question which is regarded as bearing on the problem of dating is that of the composition of the political body with which Phormisios lodged his proposal. Usener —basing himself on par. 5 where he takes ταύτης to mean πολιτείας, and on the alleged fact that the orator addresses himself throughout the speech to property owners only— maintains that there was a provisional government after the return of the exiles, during which the ekklesia was composed of property owners. To this assembly Lysias addresses himself during the short period of provisional regime.[31] This view was accepted by Wilamowitz[32]—who quotes *Ath. Pol.* 39,6 and maintains that the Assembly was composed of the τιμήματα παρεχόμενοι mentioned there— and by some other scholars.[33] However, γῆ not πολιτεία is meant in ὑμῖν τὴν ὑμετέραν ἀπέδωκεν, and ταύτης μετασχεῖν in par. 5.[34] It is true that the speaker often addresses himself to property owners. There could, however, be little doubt that the poor would at any rate vote against Phormisios; those to be influenced were the property owners. Lysias tries to exert an influence mainly on these. But he addresses himself not to them only. 'If by your votes you are to enslave yourselves' (par. 2) is directed to those in danger of losing their citizen-rights; and 'in so far as you may' in par. 5 seems to show that the outcome was not dependent on property owners only. *Ath. Pol.* 39,6, referred to by Wilamowitz, has nothing to do with the ekklesia, its concern is the composition of the special juridical panels for the *euthynai*-cases consequent on the restoration. They were

44

active under the restored democracy (*Ath. Pol.* 38,4); their unusual composition is possibly instructive in connection with the events which preceded the reconciliation, but it does not prove anything about the regime after the 12 of Boedromion.[35] There never was any provisional constitution (see also above, pp. 36 sqq.), and neither *Ath. Pol.* 39,6 nor the speech itself supply any definite evidence for dating. We have to fall back on Dionysios' δήμου κατελθόντος καὶ ψηφισαμένου διαλύσασθαι for what it is worth, and on some general considerations of the historical situation. Since, if we keep to Dionysios' remarks, we cannot date the proposal of Phormisios and Lysias' rejoinder much later than the 12 of Boedromion, there seem to be two main possibilities of dating: either before, or shortly after the psephisma of Teisamenos. If the first is correct, the motion of Phormisios was submitted to the Assembly (either directly, as for some time the ekklesia was the only functioning organ, or through the Council); if the latter suggestion is correct, the proposal was lodged with the Council and the nomothetai, and would come under the cover of: ἐξεῖναι δὲ καὶ ἰδιώτῃ τῷ βουλομένῳ ... συμβουλεύειν ὅ τι ἂν ἀγαθὸν ἔχῃ περὶ τῶν νόμων of the Decree of Teis. Historical circumstances do not seem to exclude any of these possibilities. Although the decree of Teisamenos provided for additional legislation within democracy (above, pp. 37 sqq.), Phormisios' proposal was no such 'high treason' as is alleged by Lysias. If we take Dionysios' γῆν ἔχουσι as a shortened expression for γῆν ἢ οἰκίαν,[36] the number of 5000 excluded would perhaps be

45

somewhat exaggerated,[37] and Phormisios' proposal would appear as a rather slight restriction of the democratic franchise. On the other hand extension of franchise was topical before the decree of Teisamenos, immediately after the return, when Thrasybulos submitted to the ekklesia his proposal for granting citizen-rights to all non-citizens who fought on the side of the democrats.[38] Phormisios' motion might well have been a counter-stroke calculated to hold in check the democrats.[39]

Already Dionysios of Halikarnassos (or his authority) had his doubts concerning the question of the original form of Lys. 34 ($εἰ\ μὲν\ οὖν\ ἐρρήθη\ τότε,\ ἄδηλον$). The fact that it is written as if it were an actual speech [40] does not prove that it was ever delivered, nor that it was written to be delivered in the Assembly. It might as well be taken to indicate that Lysias was successful in writing a pamphlet in the form of a political speech. Nor is $ἐγὼ\ μὲν\ οὖν\ .\ .\ .\ ⟨οὔτε\ οὐσία⟩\ οὔτε$ $γένει\ ἀπελαυνόμενος$, par. 3 (cf. Dionysios' $τῶν\ ἐπισήμων$ $τινὶ\ καὶ\ πολιτευομένων$ which derives from this passage), sufficient proof in this connection. Putting the rejection of Phormisios' proposal into the mouth of an imaginary well-to-do and influential citizen who was among the exiles would seem to be an ingenious device in a pamphlet calculated to exert influence on the propertied classes. On the other hand there is nothing in the fragment which would preclude taking Lys. 34 as an actual speech. In this case it could have been delivered by some democratic politician, and then published as a political credo of the democrats even after Phormisios' proposal was turned down.

We seem to be on somewhat firmer ground when we turn to the question of the title of Lys. 34. In modern editions it usually bears the name: περὶ τοῦ μὴ καταλῦσαι τὴν πάτριον πολιτείαν Ἀθήνησιν. That is based on Dionysios' ὑπόθεσιν δ᾽ περιείληφε, with the above quoted words following. Ὑπόθεσις does not, strictly speaking, mean 'title', it may have been used here in the sense in which it is used by Dionysios in, for instance, de Lys. 20,22,29 (cf. also Pomp. 3,2), i.e. 'subject', 'subject-matter'. But how could Dionysios know that the subject of Lysias, or. 34, was περὶ τοῦ μὴ καταλῦσαι τὴν πάτριον πολιτείαν? The term πάτριος πολιτεία does not occur in the preserved part of the speech. Dionysios could well have inferred that it was περὶ τοῦ μὴ καταλῦσαι τὴν δημοκρατίαν (that was, as Lysias alleges, what Phormisios' proposal amounted to), not that it was περὶ πατρίου πολιτείας. Πάτριος πολιτεία, πάτριοι νόμοι, ἀρχαῖοι νόμοι were, as we have seen, sometimes used by the democrats in the sense of demokratia; but π.π. and δημοκρατία were not simply interchangeable terms, certainly not so for Dionysios. Since we cannot apparently make Dionysios of Halikarnassos responsible for changing δημοκρατία into πάτριος πολιτεία, he must have found it (a) either in the now lost part of the speech, or (b) as a title in his copy of the speech. Although Blass seems to be right in supposing, in view of the general trend of Lysias' argument, that only a small portion of the speech is lost to us, the words πάτριος πολιτεία might have occurred in the final sentences of the peroration. Again, the copies of Lysias' speeches used by Dionysios of Halikarnassos are known to have been supplied with titles: cf. e.g. *de Lys.* 20 (ὁ λόγος . . . ἐπιγραφόμενος κατὰ Διογείτονος). It seems to be perfectly possible that Lys. or. 34 bore on its publication the name: περὶ τοῦ μὴ καταλῦσαι τὴν πάτριον πολιτείαν ᾿Αθήνησιν, and that Dionysios found such an ἐπιγραφή in his copy of the speech. Πάτριος πολιτεία is used here, as πάτριοι νόμοι in Thuc. 8,76,6, against the moderates: it denotes democracy with full franchise.[41]

NOTES TO CHAPTER II

1. The idea that sound judgement of the demos in politics compares favourably with that of their opponents of the educated class occurs both in Thukydides' report of the Assembly in Samos and in Thrasybulos' speech (cf. Thuc. 8,76,6 with *Hell.* 2,4,41). Possibly some of Thrasybulos' ideas are embodied in Thukydides' relation.

2. Cf. Lipsius, *Phil. Woch.* 1917, col. 906.

3. Lipsius, col. 909.

4. Cf. Ferguson, *Classical Studies presented to E. Capps* (1936), p. 146.

5. Cf. Ferguson, pp. 145–6.

6. Perhaps a small commission of 10 if Sluiter's reading οἱ δέ(κα) (cf. Makkink, *Andokides' eerste Rede*, 1932, ad loc.) is correct; cf. Busolt-Swoboda, p. 920, n. 1; Schoell, *Comment. Momms.* (1877), p. 467; Meyer, *G.d.A.* 5, p. 215; see also Kahrstedt, *Klio* 31 (1938), p. 10 (for a different view cf. Von der Mühll, *Hermes* 68, 1933, p. 117).

7. Ferguson, *op. cit.*, 144 sq.

8. Teisamenos himself, and Nikomachos, were among them, cf. Lys. 30,28; see Ferguson, p. 145, for this board as anagrapheis; cf. also Gantzer, *Verfassungs-und Gesetzrevision* (1894), p. 61; Smith, *Ath. polit. commissions* (1920), pp. 71 sqq.; Kahrstedt, *Klio* 31 (1938), p. 10 sq.

9. Oliver, *Hesperia* 4 (1935), pp. 1 sqq.

10. Cf. Ferguson, pp. 144 sqq.; and *ibid.*, pp. 146–7: 'The fine new publication in the Royal Stoa did not need to be destroyed or mutilated. Without chiselling in substitutes, the additions could be incised on the wall as the decree of Teisamenos prescribed.'

11. Cf. Ferguson, p. 144, and his interpretation of Lys. 30.

12. Cf. Hirzel, *op. cit.*, pp. 37 sqq.

13. Cf. Dem. 24,56; see Calhoun, *C.P.* 13 (1918), pp. 181 sqq.; Dorjahn, *Political Forgiveness in old Athens* (1946), p. 24 sq.; Lenschau, *P.W.* 20,1, col. 542.

14. Recently again in Bury, *History of Greece*, 3 ed. (1951), p. 513; cf. also Atkinson, *Athenian legisl. procedure* (1939), p. 44.

15. *Op. cit.*, Appendix 4.

16. *Op. cit.*, pp. 49–50: '... non priscos leges Solonis et Draconis sed corpus iuris democratiae saeculi quinti ...'; cf. Gilbert, *Beiträge z. inn. Gesch. Athens* (1877), p. 331.

17. Cf. e.g. *Sch. Aesch.* 1,39.

18. For the use of κατὰ τὰ πάτρια, πάτριον, π.π in some international agreements cf. the sources quoted in n. 16, ch. 3; for some other occurrences of these terms see e.g.: Syll.³ 390, 15 sqq.: τάς τε πόλεις ἐλευθερώσας καὶ τοὺς νόμους ἀποδοὺς [κ]αὶ τὴμ πάτριομ πολιτείαμ πᾶσιν καταστήσας (viz. Ptolemy II; about 280 B.C.; decree of the synod of Nesiotai); Syll.³ 572, 16 sqq.: νόμοις τοῖς πατρίοις καὶ ὑπάρχουσιν χρῆσθαι (about 201 B.C.; Philip V to Nisyra); Syll.³ 434–5, 15 sqq.: διὰ το[ὺς κ]αταλύειν ἐπιχειροῦντας τούς τε νόμους καὶ τὰς πατρίους ἑκάστοις πολιτείας ... (decree concerning Greek alliance against Antigonos Gonatas; opening of the Chremonidean war); Hell. 6,5,6; Polyb. 2,47,3; 2,70,1; 4,25,7; 4,35,8; 4,81,12–14; 5,9,8–9; 9,36,4; Syll.³ 819 (A.D.I.; π.π. stands for democracy); see also Arist. *Pol.* 1267B, 1 sqq. (diobelia as πάτριον); Syll.³ 359 (fourth century B.C.); Tod, no. 151, 15 sqq. (alliance between Athens and Thracian kings, 357 B.C.: τὸμ φό]ρον τὸμ πάτριον); Lys. 28,5 (ἀρχαῖοι νόμοι as applying to the phoros of the Athenian empire). (Some of the above usages qualified by πάτριον are demonstrably recent enough.) See also e.g. *Pol.* 1268B, 25 sqq.; *Ath. Pol.* 39,5; Hdt. 3,82,5 and 3,80,5.

19. Cf. ch. 3, n. 16.

20. Plut. *Demetr.* 10,1–2: ἀπέδωκε (i.e. Demetrios Poliork.) τὴν πάτριον πολιτείαν ... Ἀθηναῖοι δ' ἀπολαβόντες τὴν δημοκρατίαν ... κτλ.; Diod.

49

20,46,3: ὁ μὲν οὖν δῆμος . . . παραδόξως ἐκομίσατο τὴν πάτριον πολιτείαν. Cf. also n. 18. (See also Dimitrakos, *Demetrios Poliorketes und Athen*, 1937, pp. 25 sqq.)

21. If there is any archaizing tendency in the Pseph.-Teis. it appears rather in the Areiopagos clause than in the κατὰ τὰ πάτρια clause and Solon-Drakon clause. Though the right of supervision extended to the Areiopagos was, probably, provisional: cf. Ferguson, *Klio* 4 (1904), pp. 9–10, n. 5; Kahrstedt, *Klio* 30 (1937), p. 28.

22. Cf. Blass, *Att. Bereds.* 1², p. 451.

23. The figure of 5000 citizens excluded was found by Dionysios either in the non-preserved part of the speech, or in his authority, possibly the *Atthis* of Philochoros; cf. Blass, p. 450; Meyer, *G.d.A.* 5, p. 217 sq.; Lenschau, *P.W.* 20,1, col. 543; cf. also Meyer, *Forsch.* 2, p. 176.

24. Cf. especially par. 1, where 'twice' refers to the moderates' constitutional proposals of 411 and 404 respectively, and par. 2. See e.g. Cloché, *Restauration démocratique* (1915), pp. 155, 424 sqq.; Gernet-Bizos, *Lysias* (ed. Budé, 1926) 2, p. 205; Lenschau, *op. cit.*, col. 544; Meyer, *G.d.A.* 5, p. 216; Ferckel, *Lysias und Athen* (1937), p. 48; Mathieu, *R.E.G.* 40 (1927), p. 110.

25. Cf. *Ath. Pol.* 34,3.

26. Cf. e.g. Gernet-Bizos, p. 206 sq.; Mathieu, *op. cit.*; Ferckel, p. 50.

27. *Op. cit.*, p. 280 sq., 420 sqq.; cf. also Grosser, *Jahrb. f. Kl. Phil.* 101 (1870), p. 597.

28. *Op. cit.*, col. 543 sq.

29. *Hell.* 2,2,2.

30. Lamb, *Lysias* (L.C.L., 1930), p. 691.

31. *Jahrb. f. Kl. Phil.* 107 (1873), pp. 145 sqq., especially 164 sqq. (according to Usener the democrats took a strictly legalistic attitude; the regime established after the fall of democracy in 404 was being regarded as legal, and to it they felt themselves obliged to stick for the time being).

32. *Ar. u. Ath.* 2, pp. 223 sqq.

33. Cf. e.g. Gernet-Bizos, *op. cit.*, p. 207 sq.; Lamb, *op. cit.*, p. 693.

34. Cf. Blass, *op. cit.*, p. 451n.; Ed. Meyer, *Forsch.* 2, p. 177n.; Cloché, *op. cit.*, pp. 422 sqq.

35. For a more detailed discussion see Fuks in *Mnemosyne* for 1953.

36. Wilamowitz, *op. cit.*, p. 227.

37. Wilamowitz, *op. cit.*, p. 229.

38. *Ath. Pol.* 40,2 (cf. *Hell.* 2,4,25; Ps.-Plut. *Lys.* 835F); see Cloché, *op. cit.*, pp. 447 sqq.; Ferckel, *op. cit.*, pp. 26 sqq.

39. Dionysios' expression γνώμην εἰσηγήσατο (*de Lys.* 32) would seem to fit better this supposition.

40. Dionysios, l.c.

41. For two additional sources in which π.π. is used in the sense of democracy cf. ch. I, n. 37 (Dem. 23,205); and ch. III, pp. 63 sqq. (Diod. 14,3,3). [Addendum to pp. 34–40: Hignett's excellent discussion, *A History of the Athenian Constitution* (1952), pp. 300 sqq., appeared after this has been set in type.]

Chapter III

ΠΑΤΡΙΟΣ ΠΟΛΙΤΕΙΑ
FROM THE PEACE-TREATY OF 404 B.C.
TO THE FIRST PHASE OF THE RULE
OF THE THIRTY

Accorᴅɪɴɢ to Arist. *Ath. Pol.* 34,3 and Diod. 14,3,2;6 the conditions of the peace-treaty of 404 B.C. included a clause on the Athenian constitution, which was to be a πάτριος πολιτεία, and some constitutional change is implied also in Lys. 12,70. No such clause is referred to in other sources which relate the conditions of peace: Plut. *Lysan.* 14,8; Andoc. 3, 11–12, cf. 3,31; 3,39; 1,80; Xen. *Hell.* 2,2,20; Diod. 13,107,4.

Roughly speaking, those of the sources which include the π.π. clause do not supply details of the treaty, while in the others a detailed account of the peace-treaty is given.[1] We shall try to reconstruct the conditions of the treaty on the basis of the sources which supply detailed reference before we discuss the question whether a clause concerning the 'ancestral constitution' was included in it. Plutarch quotes in *Lysan.* 14,8 the conditions prescribed in a δόγμα of the Spartan ephors. The question of whence this document comes to Plutarch (both Theopompos and Ephoros were proposed) [2] does not seem to be of great importance in this connection. Whatever Plutarch's source, the dialect and style of the relation seem to show that we have before us the original dogma of the ephors, or an account closely based on it; [3] and it is verified by what we know from other sources on the details of the ratified treaty. It is not the treaty itself; details such as the number of ships to be retained by Athens were left for decision on the spot; but since the conditions of the ephors were accepted by Athens this dogma is to be supposed to be on all essential points the basis of the treaty. The conditions were: (a) the Long Walls and the fortifications of the Piraeus were to be pulled down; (b) Athens was to lose her foreign possessions; (c) all exiles were to be allowed to return; (d) the number of ships to be left to Athens was to be decided on the spot. All these points are attested to by Andokides, who refers in 3,11–12 to the treaty of 404 when speaking in 392–1 in favour of the peace with Sparta: [4] (a) tally almost exactly (cf. also 3,31; 39 and 1,80); for (b) Andokides has Λῆμνον δὲ καὶ Ἴμβρον καὶ Σκῦρον . . . ἔχειν τοὺς ἔχοντας (cf. 3, 14; also Aesch. 2,76). It may be supposed either that in the final draft of the treaty the northern islands were mentioned as being lost to Athens, or that although they were not singled out in it, Andokides stresses here the case of Lemnos, Imbros and Skyros since their position was to be expressly reversed in the treaty discussed in 392–1. As Andokides' main point is the benevolence of Sparta, the singling out of the northern islands may derive from the situation of his day, not from a specification in the treaty of 404.[5] Clause (c) is confirmed by Andokides' account (l.c., see also 3,31; 1,81), while in (d) he states the number of ships left to Athens as 12, thus recording the decision taken on the spot and included in the ratified treaty. Andokides refers to the original stele on which the peace-treaty of 404 was recorded (3,12), and there is no reason to doubt that he had seen it and knew the treaty well. The account of Xenophon, *Hell.* 2,2,20, corresponds to those of Plut. *Lysan.* and Andok. with two exceptions. Xenophon adds the clause: τὸν αὐτὸν ἐχθρὸν καὶ φίλον νομίζοντας Λακεδαιμονίοις ἕπεσθαι καὶ κατὰ γῆν καὶ κατὰ θάλατταν ὅποι ἂν ἡγῶνται and omits clause (b) of the dogma. The ἐχθρόν-φίλον clause occurs frequently in treaties of offensive and defensive alliance (e.g. I.G.[2] 1,71,20; 90,18; Thuc. 1,44,1; 3,75,1).[6] Although not restricted to leagues it seems to have been characteristic of them.[7] It was one of the corner-stones of the Delian League,[8] and it is likely that it 'formed a part of the treaties embodying the constitution of the Peloponnesian League'.[9] The treaty of 404 seems to be the first known evidence—in connection with the Peloponnesian League—of a one-sided ἐχθρόν-φίλον clause, according to which one of the contracting parties owes obedience to the other. However, whether there were previous instances or not, this is not isolated. It occurs in the peace-treaty concluded in 379 B.C. between Sparta and Olynthos in a somewhat similar situation (*Hell.* 5,3,26; cf. Diod. 15,23,3). And

54

there must have been more such treaties in the Peloponnesian League, since at the peace-negotiations at Sparta in 371 B.C. Autokles the Athenian criticizes Sparta for imposing the ἔπεσθαι clause on her allies (*Hell.* 6,3,7).[10] Thus the ἐχθρόν-φίλον-ἔπεσθαι clause referred to by Xenophon indicates the inclusion of Athens (as a subject ally) in the Peloponnesian League.[11] There arises the question whether this clause may be regarded as forming part of the treaty of 404 although it does not appear either in Plut. *Lysan.* or in Andok. With regard to the dogma of the ephors, one would not suppose that such a clause could have been omitted by Plutarch or his source and still believe in the documentary value of *Vit. Lysan.* 14,8. We have, however, to bear in mind that the dogma states the Spartan conditions only; it does not give the final peace-treaty. Now, we know from Xen. *Hell.* 2,2,11 that when first approaching Sparta in connection with the peace the Athenians offered 'to become allies of the Lacedaemonians (σύμμαχοι εἶναι) while they retained their Walls and the Piraeus'. The latter proposal was rejected by the Spartans; hence the demolition of the Walls does appear as one of the Spartan conditions. On the other hand the first proposal was accepted by Sparta, and therefore does not appear in the dogma, which states only the Spartan conditions *sine quibus non*. It could not, however, have been omitted from the final peace-treaty when it came to be drafted. Andokides' silence in this respect does not seem to invalidate these conclusions as he does not propose to quote the treaty in full, but only what is relevant to his immediate purpose. The stressing of Athens' subjection to Sparta—reversed by the naval victory of Konon and the rebuilding of the Walls—did not perhaps seem to Andokides apt to strengthen his argument in favour of the peace-proposals of 392-1. If this is correct we have in Xenophon's account the fifth—(e)—of the conditions of the peace-treaty. The omission of clause (b) by Xenophon may be due to carelessness, or the fall of the Athenian empire could have been regarded by Xenophon as too evident to his readers to need repetition. The last detailed account of the treaty is Diod. 13,107,4. It repeats fairly closely all the points we derive from the sources surveyed so far with the omission of clause (c).[12] Diodoros' account of the treaty is supposed to be based on Ephoros, and it is sometimes held (cf. Meyer, G.d.A. 4, p. 666) that Xenophon was here Ephoros' source. The latter does not seem to me probable. Diodoros' account of (a) is closer to the dogma than that of any other source; it repeats the σκέλη while others speak of τείχη; (b) is again closer to Lysan. 14 than either Xen. or Andok. For (e) a shortened version of the clause preserved in Xen. is given (Λακεδαιμονίοις ἡγεμόσι χρῆσθαι). Thus, it seems to be possible that Ephoros (Diod.) has not here used Xen. at all, practically certain that he knew of the treaty more than could have been read in the Hellenika of Xenophon. In this case the independent value of Diodoros' account seems to be enhanced.

All these clauses—(a) to (e)—are commonly taken to have been included in the peace-treaty. Busolt, however, supposes that there were *two* documents, a peace-treaty and a separate treaty of alliance 'as in 421' (Busolt, G.G. 3,2, p. 1635,1, cf. Busolt-Swoboda, p. 911n.). However, the alliance which followed the peace-treaty of 421 was concluded between equals, while in 404 Athens had to accept an imposed peace (Andoc. 3,12; cf. 11). The difference is fundamental, and no conclusions drawn from 421 seem to be justifiable with regard to 404. Busolt does not disbelieve the genuineness of clause (e), but since he does not find it either in the highly reliable Plut. *Lysan.* 14,8 or in Andokides, he concludes that it must have been included in another document. But, as already pointed out, Plut. *Lysan.* and Andok.—valuable as far as they go—cannot, by their very nature, warrant completeness. Furthermore, in the peace-treaty between Sparta and Olynthos, concluded in a situation resembling that of 404, the ἐχθρόν-φίλον-ἔπεσθαι clause was included (above, p. 54). There is therefore no need to suppose that clause (e) does not belong to the peace-treaty.

So far we have ignored such sources as have the establishment of a πάτριος πολιτεία at Athens as one of the conditions of the treaty of 404: Arist. *Ath. Pol.* 34,3; Diod. 14,3,2, cf. 6. Can it be that there was such an additional clause in the treaty? Plut. *Lysan.* 14,8 is close to the dogma of the ephors on which the treaty was based, and the absence in it of the π.π. clause would seem to be rather difficult to explain, especially as general political questions were certainly within the competence of the ephors rather

57

than of the commander in the field.[13] Andokides, although not reproducing the treaty in full, goes back to the original stele; Ephoros (in Diod. 13,107,4) seems to have had a good, perhaps a documentary knowledge of the treaty. The same applies—despite one omission—to Xenophon. Whatever the limitations of each separate source, their cumulative value is considerable. They might have omitted single phrases or details [14] but hardly an important clause. It seems therefore safer to assume that a mistaken tradition is embodied in *Ath. Pol.* and Diod. than to attribute a grave omission to the sources which supply detailed reference to the conditions of the treaty.[15] *Ath. Pol.* 34,2–3 and Diod. 14,3,2–14,4,1 are the only sources which state that an ancestral constitution clause was included in the treaty (τῆς εἰρήνης γενομένης αὐτοῖς ἐφ᾽ ᾧ τε πολιτεύσονται τὴν πάτριον πολιτείαν . . . *Ath. Pol.* 34,3; συνθήκας . . . καθ᾽ ἃς ἔδει τὰ τείχη . . . καθελεῖν καὶ τῇ πατρίῳ πολιτείᾳ χρῆσθαι . . . Diod. 14,3,2). Also, they are the only sources which have a description of a clash between political parties in connection with the constitution, subsequent to the conclusion of the peace. Furthermore, Aristotle and Diodoros are the only sources in which the Thirty are said to have been established by Lysandros in face of Theramenes' opposition (cf. *Ath. Pol.* 34,2 with Diod. 14,3,5–7). The impression that Aristotle and Diodoros are here basing themselves on a common source seems to be confirmed by the similarities in the following passages:

Λυσάνδρου δὲ προσθεμένου τοῖς ὀλιγαρχικοῖς (i.e. against

58

Theramenes) *καταπλαγεὶς ὁ δῆμος ἠναγκάσθη χειροτονεῖν τὴν ὀλιγαρχίαν* . . . *Ath. Pol.* 34,3. *Διόπερ ὅ τε Θηραμένης καὶ ὁ δῆμος καταπλαγεὶς ἠναγκάζετο χειροτονίᾳ καταλῦσαι τὴν δημοκρατίαν* . . . Diod. 14,3,7. There seems to be a distinct apologetic tendency in the source of *Ath. Pol.* and Diod. Theramenes and his 'ancestral constitution' were for this source 'good', the Thirty Tyrants and their taskmaster Lysandros 'bad'. Now, Theramenes was closely connected with the rule of the Thirty. He was an influential statesman at Athens in the period after the peace-treaty and before the election of the Thirty; he was the central figure in the ekklesia in which the rule of the Thirty was established (below, pp. 70 sqq.); and his influence was, I think, considerable also in the first phase of the rule of the Thirty, when there seems to have existed a collaboration between the extremists and the moderates (below, pp. 72 sqq.). The purpose of the source of Aristotle and Diodoros was, it seems, to disconnect Theramenes from the Thirty and to save him from the odium incurred by their rule. That is achieved by *ante-dating* Theramenes' breach with the extremists and Lysandros. It occurred— according to this pro-Theramenean version—immediately after the peace-treaty, not (as it did in fact) some months after the inauguration of the rule of the Thirty. The unknown authority of Arist. and Diod. wants to eliminate not only the period of the collaboration of Theramenes with the extremists during the rule of the Thirty, and his prominent rôle in its establishment, but also the period of

Theramenes' collaboration with the oligarchs during about five months after the peace and before the Assembly περὶ πολιτείας (cf. below, pp. 63 sqq.). To achieve that he had to have the breach between Theramenes and the extremists and Lysandros as close as possible to the peace-treaty, in fact he puts it almost immediately after it. *Post hoc* seems to have become with him *propter hoc*, and the breach is implied to have been caused by a clause concerning constitution allegedly included in the peace-treaty. A misinterpretation of an expression or a formula which may have appeared in the peace-treaty might have contributed to the origin of this version. Terms such as κατὰ τὰ πάτρια, τὸ πάτριον, and πατρ. πολιτεία occur not infrequently in Greek international agreements. They do not imply any return to an 'ideal' or 'lost' constitution but mean usually that the contracting parties guarantee (either unilaterally or multilaterally as the case may be) the internal autonomy, whatever be the constitution of the state.[16] In the peace-treaty between Sparta and Argos of 418 B.C., there occurs the formula: τὰς δὲ πόλιας τὰς ἐν Πελοποννάσῳ καὶ μικρὰς καὶ μεγάλας αὐτονόμως εἶμεν πάσας καττὰ πάτρια, and αὐτονόμοι καὶ αὐτοπόλεις δίκας διδόντες ... καττὰ πάτρια is found in the instrument of alliance between these two states.[17] In his speech in Akanthos, Brasidas stresses the right of the states of Greece to live according to their ancestral constitutional practice (τὸ πάτριον) (Thuc. 4,86,4). That is the official policy of Sparta, not only Brasidas' personal view. Lysandros' establishing of oligarchic dekarchies was a deviation from this policy. The opposition between the declared policy of Sparta to preserve the 'ancestral constitutions' and Lysandros' approach is clear from *Hell.* 3,4,2 (cf. also Plut. *Ages.* 6,2), where Lysandros is said to have wished in 396 to accompany Agesilaos to Asia 'in order that he might re-establish, in concert with him, the governments of Ten, which had been appointed by him in the several cities, and which had been abolished by the ephors, who ordered the people to return to their ancestral constitutions (τὰς πατρίους πολιτείας παρήγγειλαν)'. Whether the correct reasons of Lysandros' eagerness to accompany Agesilaos are here given, and whether the dekarchies could have been abolished by a proclamation of the ephors,[18] does not concern us here. In any event there are no sufficient grounds for doubting that the elements in Spartan government opposed to Lysandros propounded the declared policy of π.π.[19] Although in later times Sparta deviated in practice from this policy, which was one of the basic principles of the Peloponnesian League, she clung in theory to guaranteeing the internal autonomy to every Greek state.[20] Thus such an expression as κατὰ τὰ πάτρια, or αὐτονόμους κατὰ τὰ πάτρια, or even πολιτεύεσθαι τὴν πάτριον πολιτείαν might have occurred in the final draft of the treaty of 404. If it did occur, it must have been the normal guarantee on the part of Sparta not to interfere in Athens' domestic affairs; it was not an instruction to adopt any definite constitution, as it appears in *Ath. Pol.* and Ephoros.

It cannot be known with certainty whether we have here a mistake or a deliberate misrepresentation. It might have been a mere mistake originating in putting the party-political clash immediately after the peace and in the misunderstanding of a phrase in the treaty. On the other hand the possibility of a deliberate misrepresentation is to be reckoned with. It is alleged in the strongly anti-Theramenean version of events given by Lysias that a clause concerning a change of the constitution was suggested to Sparta by Theramenes and included in the treaty (Lys. 12,70). The character of the change is not specified, but the impression Lysias attempts to create is that the oligarchy of the Thirty was secured by Theramenes in the treaty.[21] The common source of Aristotle and Ephoros may be combating such a tendency by stressing that Theramenes wanted to *avert* the oligarchy by faithful implementation of the peace-treaty which, allegedly, has foreseen for Athens the π.π. The pro-Theramenean writer might have considered that to represent Theramenes as true both to his ideal of π.π. and to the peace-treaty, brought to naught by the extremists and Lysandros, was serving his apologetic tendency. At any rate we have to conclude that no specific constitution was imposed on Athens by the treaty, and that the tendency of the common source of Aristotle and Ephoros was distinctly pro-Theramenean.

This apologetic trend would seem to be in accord with what we should expect of Androtion.[22] The use of Androtion's *Atthis* in the historical part of the *Ath. Pol.* is widely accepted, and the utilization by Aristotle of his narrative for the period of the Thirty was convincingly demonstrated by Busolt;[23] he also points to the frequent parallels between the accounts in *Ath. Pol.* and Diod. and other sources dependent on Ephoros. In view of this it seems to be highly probable—though not fully demonstrable—that Androtion's *Atthis* was the common source used by both Aristotle and Ephoros (Diod.)[24] in the passages under discussion.[25]

Although mistakenly connecting the question of π.π. with the treaty, the common source of Aristotle and Ephoros has considerable value for the appreciation of the problem of π.π. in Athens' internal politics after the peace and before the establishment of the Thirty. The general scheme of its story, recoverable from the fuller account of Ephoros (Diod.), and recognizable in the compressed passage of Aristotle, seems to have been, approximately, as follows: (*a*) party-political discussion about Athens' constitution, connected with the question of π.π., starts after the conclusion of peace (Diod. 14,3,3; cf. *Ath. Pol.* 34,3 from οἱ μέν ... to ... ἐζήτουν); (*b*) the difficulties of the oligarchs (Diod. 14,3,3; not specified in *Ath. Pol.*); (*c*) Lysandros summoned by the extremists to help in overcoming the democratic regime (Diod. 14,3,4–5; *Ath. Pol.*: Lysandros and the oligarchs, 34,2 from ἐξ ... to ... τοιῷδε); (*d*) Assembly convoked; Lysandros presses against Theramenes' strong opposition for establishing an oligarchy (Diod. 14,3,5–7; *Ath. Pol.* 34,3 ... μάλιστα

63

Θηραμένης. Λυσάνδρου δὲ κτλ.; that refers undoubtedly to the Assembly described in fuller detail in Diod.); (e) the Thirty Tyrants established (Diod. 14,3,7–14,4,1; *Ath. Pol.* 34,3 records the name of the proposer of the decree). In spite of some fundamental differences between Lysias and the trend which manifests itself in Diod. and Arist. we find in Lysias' orations 12 and 13 all of the above stated points with the exception of (a). For (b) we have in Lysias the story of the democratic counter-action headed by the strategoi and the taxiarchoi (13,5 sqq., 17 sqq.) and the story of the activities of the oligarchic ephors (12,43 sqq.). They make clear the difficulties encountered by the opposition in overcoming the democratic regime; (c) Lysandros is summoned by Theramenes (12,71); (d) Assembly on Constitution in which Theramenes and Lysandros speak; under Lysandros' pressure the democratic opposition is silenced (12,73 sqq.); (e) the Thirty established in office according to the decree of Drakontides (12,76, cf. 73).

Those are, I believe, the events of about five months from the conclusion of the peace-treaty (end of April 404) to the beginning of the rule of the Thirty (end of September 404).[26] The place of the question of π.π. during these five months may be conveniently discussed in connection with the points referred to above.

(a) Both Aristotle and Ephoros (Diod.) refer to a party-political clash at Athens over the constitutional question; according to both it starts after the peace and derives from it. Although there are grounds for questioning the connec-

64

tion between the treaty of peace and the question of π.π. there is no reason for doubting that the 'ancestral constitution' again became topical after the conclusion of the peace.

Theramenes seems to have become, in view of his rôle in the negotiations with Sparta, a most influential figure at Athens, and the time might well have seemed to him to be ripe for another attempt to realize his ideal of a moderate polity, avowedly a return to the π.π. Theramenes is closely connected with the re-occurrence of the question of π.π. in both Aristotle and Diodoros. But, when we turn to the question of the rôle that he had played in this connection, and the attitude of the Athenian parties to the problem of π.π., we find far-reaching differences between Aristotle and Diodoros:

Τῆς εἰρήνης γενομένης αὐτοῖς ἐφ᾽ ᾧ τε πολιτεύσονται τὴν πάτριον πολιτείαν οἱ μὲν δημοτικοὶ διασῴζειν ἐπειρῶντο τὸν δῆμον, τῶν δὲ γνωρίμων οἱ μὲν ἐν ταῖς ἑταιρείαις ὄντες καὶ τῶν φυγάδων οἱ μετὰ τὴν εἰρήνην κατελθόντες ὀλιγαρχίας ἐπεθύμουν, οἱ δ᾽ ἐν ἑταιρείᾳ μὲν οὐδεμίᾳ συγκατεσθῶτες ἄλλως δὲ δοκοῦντες οὐδενὸς ἐπιλείπεσθαι τῶν πολιτῶν τὴν πάτριον πολιτείαν ἐζήτουν. ὧν ἦν μὲν καὶ Ἀρχῖνος καὶ Ἄνυτος καὶ Κλειτοφῶν καὶ Φορμίσιος καὶ ἕτεροι πολλοί, προειστήκει δὲ μάλιστα Θηραμένης. Λυσάνδρου δὲ προσθεμένου τοῖς ὀλιγαρχικοῖς καταπλαγεὶς ὁ δῆμος ἠναγκάσθη χειροτονεῖν τὴν ὀλιγαρχίαν.—Ath. Pol. 34,3.

Ἐποιήσαντο συνθήκας . . . καθ᾽ ἃς ἔδει τὰ τείχη τῆς πόλεως καθελεῖν καὶ τῇ πατρίῳ πολιτείᾳ χρῆσθαι. καὶ τὰ μὲν τείχη περιεῖλον, περὶ δὲ τῆς πολιτείας πρὸς ἀλλήλους διεφέροντο. οἱ γὰρ τῆς ὀλιγαρχίας ὀρεγόμενοι τὴν παλαιὰν κατάστασιν ἔφασαν διανείμασ-

65

θαι, καθ' ἣν παντελῶς ὀλίγοι τῶν πολλῶν προειστήκεσαν· οἱ δὲ πλεῖστοι δημοκρατίας ὄντες ἐπιθυμηταὶ τὴν τῶν πατέρων πολιτείαν προεφέροντο, καὶ ταύτην ἀπέφηναν ὁμολογουμένως οὖσαν δημοκρατίαν ... ἀντειπόντος δὲ τοῦ Θηραμένους (against Lysandros) ὅτι τῇ πατρίῳ συνεφώνησε χρήσεσθαι πολιτείᾳ ... ὅ τε Θηραμένης καὶ ὁ δῆμος καταπλαγεὶς ἠναγκάζετο χειροτονίᾳ καταλῦσαι τὴν δημοκρατίαν.—Diod. 14,3,2–3 and 6–7.

According to Aristotle there is only one party that strives after establishing the π.π.: the middle group of Theramenes with which he evidently sympathizes. The oligarchs—the 'club-men' and among them prominently the returned exiles patronized by Lysandros—want oligarchy. The democrats want to save democracy.[27] In Diod. the democrats and the moderates, more exactly the democrats and Theramenes, are conflated into one; on the other side stand the extremists. Both sides claim the π.π. to be their ideal. To the extremists it is oligarchy, to the democrats and Theramenes the democratic regime. Now, the triple division in Athenian politics is adhered to by Aristotle throughout his story of Athenian party politics during the Peloponnesian War. Though Aristotle might have inferred it from other sources, it seems probable in view of his dependence on Androtion that he follows him both with regard to the triple division and in the bias in favour of the middle-party. At any rate we cannot make Androtion responsible for the conflation of the democrats and Therameneans into one. It must have been Ephoros (Diod.) rather than Aristotle who deviated from the common source on this occasion. Ephoros' anti-Spartan bias[28] might, tentatively, be suggested as one of the causes of his corruption of the common source. Lysandros is for Ephoros the villain of the tragedy, he stands for Sparta; Theramenes— whose opposition to Lysandros was to be found in Ephoros' source (cf. *Ath. Pol.*, l.c.)—becomes consequently the hero of the piece, and symbolizes Athens. Sparta stands for oligarchy (or tyranny), Athens for democracy. Any finer distinction (as, for instance, Sparta: Lysandros versus some of the ephors and Pausanias; Athens: moderates and democrats versus each other and versus the extremists) would only blur this clear-cut picture, which seems to have been much to Ephoros' liking.[29] In addition, 'a psychological aftermath of the experience of the revolution'[30] might have here been at work. The triple division was clear to the common source, and he must have written that Theramenes opposed the oligarchy using this term in its strictly party-political sense. 'But all distinctions within the Thirty were obliterated when Critias got control, and were quickly forgotten . . . he (i.e. the apologetic source) reaped a success with posterity beyond all his intentions, for by a natural misapprehension the next generation, so far as he moulded its opinion, regarded Theramenes as the champion of the democracy.'[31]

Since to the democrats their regime was, as we have seen, πάτριος πολιτεία or πάτριοι νόμοι it is possible that they resorted to this name in 404 (as they did in 411), but that cannot be established on the authority of the corrupt passage in Diod., l.c. On the other hand, the slogan of the 'ancestral constitution' is nowhere clearly ascribed to the oligarchs except in the Diodoros passage. To accept it on *that* authority would seem to be at least risky. We have, I think, to recognize in Diodoros a distortion of the source used both by him and by Aristotle, and accept the version of the *Ath. Pol.* concerning the question of 'ancestral constitution' as closer both to the common authority and to the facts.

(*b*) All that Diodoros has to say on the party-political activity at Athens and the difficulties encountered by the anti-democratic movement comes to: ἀντιλογίας δὲ γενομένης . . . ἐπί τινας ἡμέρας, οἱ τὰς ὀλιγαρχίας αἱρούμενοι πρὸς Λύσανδρον διεπρεσβεύοντο . . . 14,3,4. This tendency to blur and shorten the period between the peace and the establishment of the Thirty derives, it seems, from Androtion; it is, however, clear (Lysias, or. 12 and 13) that there was in this period a conspiracy of the democratic strategoi and taxiarchoi, also that here belong the activities of the committee of 'ephors'. The Athenian 'ephors' (Lys. 12,43–7) came into being after the peace and the return of the oligarchic exiles, as Kritias was one of them, and the committee was still active by the date of the election of the Thirty (12,76). There is, I think, little doubt that they were a secret oligarchic 'Actions-Comité' for directing and unifying the activities of the oligarchic clubs, not, as is sometimes supposed, a governmental body.[32] On the whole the activities directed by them must have been

68

comparable to those described by Thukydides in 8,66—i.e. preparation of the ground for final change of the constitution by paralysing the normal democratic organs, terrorism, and intimidation of the general public. The name of Kritias seems to vouchsafe their oligarchic character.[33] But the moderates seem to have been in touch with them as Eratosthenes was one of the ephors. Probably both wings of the anti-democratic opposition realized that a combination of vigorous revolutionary action with propaganda (as in 411) was needed in order to overcome the Athenian demos 'used to liberty' (Thuc. 8,68,4–5; Hell. 2,3,24, Kritias' speech). The moderates, one would suppose, were prominent in propaganda, the ephors controlled other activities. At any rate there is no trace of any breach between the two wings of the anti-democratic movement in the period under consideration. And it seems that they met with rather greater difficulties than in 411. Then the democrats were completely silenced (Thuc. 8,66), now there developed a not unimportant democratic counter-movement, the conspiracy of the strategoi and the taxiarchoi (Lys. 13,5 sqq., 17 sqq., cf. 18,4–5; 30,14). The details of the story of the democratic counter-actions do not belong here.[34] In the course of the prolonged *stasis* (Lys. 12,43) the pulling down of the Long Walls came to a standstill (see p. 80, n. 14, p. 72), and the archeiresiai were not held.[35] Though after long and weary action the democratic strategoi and taxiarchoi were finally put under arrest, it must have become increasingly clear to the anti-democratic movement that time was not on their side and that things were to be brought speedily to a head. Lysandros' presence was deemed necessary to assure success. (c) It is clear from both Lysias and Diod. that Lysandros was present in the Assembly on Constitution convoked towards the end of September 404.[36] According to Lysias the ekklesia was called by Theramenes,[37] and it was Theramenes who summoned Lysandros (Lys., l.c.). According to the other version, Lysandros was invited by the extremists (Diod., l.c.). The respective tendencies of the contrasting versions are clear. Lysias wants to have Theramenes fully responsible for the establishment of the Thirty; the pro-Theramenean source wanted to disentangle Theramenes from any connection with Lysandros and the extremists. Lysandros is, accordingly, Theramenes' violent opponent in the Assembly. We shall probably never know who communicated with Lysandros on that occasion, nor is it of great importance for appreciation of Athens' internal politics, as the moderates and the extremists seem to have acted in accord before, during, and for some months after the Assembly on Constitution (below, pp. 76 sqq.).

(d) We have two accounts of the Assembly in which the Athenian democracy was abolished and the Thirty established in power: Lys. 12,71–7 and Diod. 14,3,5–14,4,1 (cf. also *Ath. Pol.* 34,3).

Lysias: (1) an Assembly on Constitution takes place in Lysandros' presence, which was secured in order to stem any opposition and to ensure docile voting (ἵνα . . . μηδεὶς ἐναντιοῖτο κτλ.); (2) Theramenes' speech: he demands giving supreme power to a board of Thirty and adopting a constitution proposed by Drakontides; (3) opposition to Theramenes' speech (ἐθορυβεῖτε κτλ.); (4) Theramenes declares that he will not be deterred by any opposition as he has wide support (πολλοὺς . . . εἰδείη τοὺς τὰ ὅμοια πράττοντας αὐτῷ), and Sparta favours his proposals; (5) Lysandros' speech: he points out that the Athenians have not carried out the conditions of the treaty [38] and threatens reprisals if Theramenes' demands are not accepted; (6) part of the democrats leave the Assembly, others remain and keep silent; by the votes of 'few and bad' Theramenes' proposals are accepted and the Thirty established in power. Ten of them were recommended by Theramenes, ten proposed by the 'ephors', and ten elected ἐκ τῶν παρόντων. (To strengthen his point Lysias refers to the defence speech of Theramenes in which he is said to have stressed his own decisive rôle in establishing the Thirty.)

Diodoros: (1) an Assembly is convoked by Lysandros (συναγαγών), who enjoins on the Athenians the entrusting of government to thirty men; (2) Theramenes opposes Lysandros; he points out that according to the treaty the Athenian constitution was to be the π.π.; (3) Lysandros contends that the treaty was broken by the Athenians, who have not pulled down the Walls. He threatens Theramenes with death if he does not cease opposing the Lacedaemonians; (4) the demos and Theramenes are compelled under duress to do as they are told. The Thirty are elected

(the psephisma was of Drakontides of Aphidna, *Ath. Pol.*
34,3); (5) admiring Theramenes' virtue and hoping that
he would put some restraint on the tyrannical oligarchs,
the demos elects Theramenes to be one of the Thirty.
There is agreement between Lys. and Diod. (Ephor.)
on the following points: that there was an Assembly
about constitution; that Theramenes and Lysandros were
the main speakers; that Athens' failure in carrying out
one of the conditions of the treaty was pointed out by
Lysandros; that proposals submitted were opposed by the
democrats; that the Thirty were chosen according to a
psephisma of Drakontides. But as regards the rôle played
by Theramenes the two versions differ fundamentally.
Both are strongly biassed. Lysias is violently anti-Theramenean; the opposite account is distinctly pro-Theramenean, and (in Diod.) anti-Spartan. Though Lysias
might have falsified some details to suit his case (cf. below,
p. 75), it is scarcely probable that he could so completely
reverse Theramenes' rôle and misrepresent the general
situation, speaking about a year and a half after the events
to an audience many of whom might have been present
in the Assembly on Constitution. To confirm his account
of Theramenes' conduct in the Assembly Lysias quotes his
speech after the impeachment. According to Lysias, Theramenes himself stressed his paramount rôle in the peace and
the establishment of the Thirty (12,77). That is not to be
found in the speech as reported in *Hell.* 2,3,35–49.
But, though the oration in *Hell.* is, I believe, based on

Theramenes' actual speech, one would not expect a full account. Whether or not the sentiments spoken of by Lysias were expressed in Theramenes' speech, it is worth noting that very similar actions are attributed to him also in Kritias' indictment (*Hell.* 2,3,28). The mode of the election of the Thirty seems to point in the same direction. Lysias' evidence was here practically never doubted, and it was recognized long ago by Scheibe [39] that it was based on the three-party division in Athenian politics. The ten of Theramenes represent the moderate group; the men recommended by the 'ephors' are to be regarded as oligarchs; while the ten chosen from among those present were meant to represent the less intransigent, one would think, democrats. This scheme can hardly be attributed to the extremists, who were least of all interested in equal representation of the three parties; it would seem, however, totally with Theramenes' politics; and he could have hoped for the support inside the Board of the Thirty, not only of his Ten but also of the Ten ἐκ τῶν παρόντων. The fact that this mode of election was accepted would seem to point to a considerable influence exerted by Theramenes in the Assembly. And, on that supposition, the main clause of the decree of Drakontides becomes understandable.

(e) Xenophon, who does not mention the name of Drakontides, says: ἔδοξε τῷ δήμῳ τριάκοντα ἄνδρας ἑλέσθαι, οἳ τοὺς πατρίους νόμους συγγράψουσι, καθ᾿ οὓς πολιτεύσουσι . . . *Hell.* 2,3,2; and in 2,3,11: αἱρεθέντες δὲ ἐφ᾿ ᾧτε συγγράψαι νόμους, καθ᾿ οὕστινας πολιτεύσοιντο, τούτους μὲν ἀεὶ ἔμελλον συγγράφειν τε καὶ ἀποδεικνύναι (Diodoros' καὶ νόμους συγγράψαι καθ' οὓς ἔμελλον πολιτεύεσθαι, 14,4,1, may be deriving from Xenophon). The language of *Hell.* 2,3,2 gives the impression of being a quotation from a psephisma.[40] It seems to justify the assumption that the Thirty were elected as *syngrapheis*.[41] Their mandate was revision of the constitution in the sense of a re-establishment of the 'ancestral laws'. *Ath. Pol.* 34,3 (cf. also *Schol. Arist. Vesp.* 157) does not supply any evidence for the contents of the decree, but *Ath. Pol.* 35,1: 'they ignored all the resolutions which had been passed relating to the organization of the constitution', may perhaps be taken as an allusion to the above clause in the *Hellenika*.[42]

Although Lys. 12,76 does not expressly ascribe the mode of election of the Thirty to the psephisma of Drakontides it might well have been included in it, as the mode of election was prescribed also in the psephisma of Pythodoros (*Ath. Pol.* 29,2) by which the 30 syngrapheis of 411 were called into being. According to Diod. 14,4,1 election of a new Council and of magistrates was envisaged in the decree (βουλήν τε καὶ τὰς ἄλλας ἀρχὰς καταστῆσαι), and *Ath. Pol.* 35,1 says that they had appointed a Council of Five Hundred and other magistracies 'out of a thousand selected candidates'. This unusual method of election might be taken as some indication that it was prescribed in the psephisma. But this is not a necessary supposition. The Thirty might have wanted to avoid a dictatorial nomination. The sentence quoted above continues 'and associating

74

with themselves . . . three hundred "lash-bearers" as attendants . . . they kept the city under their own control' (κατὰ κράτος), and *that* could hardly have been imposed on them by the decree. The Thirty did institute a new Council and magistrates (*Hell.* 2,3,11), and it is possible that Diod. (Ephor.) confuses the powers they have usurped with those legally allowed them.[43] The only source which attributes to Drakontides authorship of a definite constitution is Lysias: ἐκέλευσεν (i.e. Theramenes) ὑμᾶς τριάκοντα ἀνδράσιν ἐπιτρέψαι τὴν πόλιν καὶ τῇ πολιτείᾳ χρῆσθαι ἣν Δρακοντίδης ἀπέφαινεν . . . 12,73. Lysias' tendency seems to be plain. He has made Theramenes responsible for the treacherous slipping into the peace-treaty of a clause securing the abolition of the democratic regime (12,70); and consequently makes him carry it out in the Assembly on Constitution. This is calculated to throw on Theramenes the full responsibility for *any* aspect of the rule of the Thirty. As there is never any indication in Lysias that the Thirty acted *ultra vires*, it would appear, if we believe Lysias, that the *character* of their rule had its roots in the constitution imposed on Athens by Theramenes.[44] Unless Xenophon's evidence concerning the πάτριοι νόμοι clause is disproved we have to reject Lysias' version. They could not both have been included in the decree of Drakontides.[45] If the election of a new Council and magistrates was in fact enjoined on the Thirty, they would appear to have been conceived as both a board of *syngrapheis* and a provisional government to act until the

75

'ancestral constitution' was drafted. At any rate the drafting of an 'ancestral constitution' was either their main,[46] or, if they were only *triginta viri legibus scribundis* (as I am inclined to think), their only task.[47]

The approval of Drakontides' decree was a success of the moderates. They started after the peace to agitate for the establishment of a moderate regime using, as they did in 411, the slogan of a 'return to the ancestral constitution'. The acceptance of Drakontides' decree was not yet the realization of the goal of the moderates; but it could be regarded as a big step towards their 'ancestral constitution'. The fact that some months later the extremists turned the tables on them should not affect our appreciation of the success of the moderates in September 404.

We have some evidence that there was during the rule of the Thirty a period of collaboration between the moderates and the extremists, when there was a marked moderate influence. It is said in *Hell.* 2,3,12: πρῶτον μὲν οὓς πάντες ᾔδεσαν ἐν τῇ δημοκρατίᾳ ἀπὸ συκοφαντίας ζῶντας καὶ τοῖς καλοῖς κἀγαθοῖς βαρεῖς ὄντας . . . ὑπῆγον θανάτου· καὶ ἥ τε βουλὴ ἡδέως αὐτῶν κατεψηφίζετο οἵ τε ἄλλοι . . . οὐδὲν ἤχθοντο. In the first period: τοῖς ἐπιεικεστάτοις . . . εὐηρέστει τὰ γιγνόμενα . . . Diod. 14,4,2. The slogans under which the rule of the Thirty was inaugurated were: τῶν ἀδίκων καθαρὰν ποιῆσαι τὴν πόλιν καὶ τοὺς λοιποὺς πολίτας ἐπ' ἀρετὴν καὶ δικαιοσύνην τράπεσθαι . . . Lys. 12,5, and Theramenes' tenet of ἀρετή as the required basis for political activity (*Ath. Pol.* 36,2) seems to be recognizable here. That there was a 'moderate period' seems to be clear even from the *Ath. Pol.*, although its tendency is to disconnect the moderates from the extremists before the beginning of the rule of the Thirty (35,2-3). It is in this period that Kritias could still have been said to be τῷ Θηραμένει ὁμογνώμων τε καὶ φίλος ... *Hell.* 2,3,16.⁴⁸ The final breach between them, and the coming to power of the extremists took place about January or February 403, the accepted date of the trial of Theramenes.⁴⁹ How the oligarchs came to power we do not know. The fact seems to be that somehow the moderates (and the general public) were taken by surprise, and suddenly realized that the real power had passed to the extremist faction. The real coups d'état both in 404 and in 411 took place not on the inauguration of the rule of the Thirty and the Four Hundred respectively but after a period of constitutional rule during which there was still collaboration between the moderates and the extremists.

The last mention of π.π. in the period dealt with in this chapter is to be seen against this background: τὸ μὲν οὖν πρῶτον μέτριοι τοῖς πολίταις ἦσαν καὶ προσεποιοῦντο διοικεῖν τὴν πάτριον πολιτείαν, καὶ τούς τ᾽ Ἐφιάλτου καὶ Ἀρχεστράτου νόμους τοὺς περὶ τῶν Ἀρεοπαγιτῶν καθεῖλον ἐξ Ἀρείου πάγου καὶ τῶν Σόλωνος θεσμῶν ὅσοι διαμφισβητήσεις εἶχον, καὶ τὸ κῦρος ὃ ἦν ἐν τοῖς δικασταῖς κατέλυσαν, ὡς ἐπανορθοῦντες καὶ ποιοῦντες ἀναμφισβήτητον τὴν πολιτείαν ... *Ath. Pol.* 35,2. The abolition of democratic legislation concerning the Areiopagos, and the changes in democratic judicature, would seem to show that steps in the direction indicated by

77

the πάτριοι νόμοι clause in the Pseph.-Drakont. were being taken under the rule of the Thirty. These measures have been mentioned elsewhere (above, p. 22 sq.), the question here is why all this is described by Aristotle as a *pretext*. Now, Aristotle could hardly have said that measures calculated to re-establish the πάτριος πολιτεία were a pretext for the moderate group. It is said in *Ath Pol.* 34,3 that the only group which sought after the 'ancestral constitution' was that of the respectable men about Theramenes, who were not members of any club (cf. also 29,3 and p. 81, n. 27), and some names of men highly esteemed after the restoration are listed with his (e.g. Archinos, cf. *Ath. Pol.* 40,2). Why then does Aristotle not say that the moderates continued their attempts to establish the π.π., while to the extremists that was all a sham. The cause is, I suggest, that Aristotle has (following his source) antedated the breach between the moderates and the extremists, and has severed any connection between the Therameneans and the extremists before the establishment of the Thirty (*Ath. Pol.* 34,3, above, pp. 59 sqq.). The rule of the Thirty is to him from its outset oligarchy pure and simple (l.c.); it is never said that Theramenes or his associates were among the Thirty. Consequently, for Aristotle there cannot be any moderate period during the rule of the Thirty, and in so far as some moderate features manifest themselves they are sham activities on the part of the oligarchs calculated to hasten the achievement of their only goal—a rule of force. And that is for Aristotle the case with π.π. under the rule

78

of the Thirty. It would seem, however, that in the first period of the rule of the Thirty steps were being taken, under the influence of the moderates, to implement the πάτριοι νόμοι clause of the psephisma of Drakontides. Possibly the extremists did not yet dare, or did not care, to show opposition. The breach between the extremists and the moderates, the oligarchic coup d'état, and the death of Theramenes brought all this to nought.

NOTES TO CHAPTER III

1. For the double account in Diodoros cf. pp. 62 sq., 81 n. 25.

2. See Scala, *Staatsverträge* (1898), p. 90 sq.; cf. also Dippel, *Quae ratio intercedat inter Xen. historiam Greaec. et Plut. vitas* (1898), p. 55 sq.

3. Cf. Busolt, G.G. 3,2,1635, n. 1; Meyer, G.d.A. 4,665; Beloch, *Griech. Gesch.* 2,1,428, n. 3; for some linguistic comment cf. Smits, *Plutarchus' Leven van Lysander* (1939), pp. 151 sqq.

4. The speech was delivered at Athens, probably in winter 392-1, after Andokides' return from his mission to Sparta; Beloch, 3,2, p. 219; Griffith, *Historia* 1 (1950), p. 242 sq.

5. Since the kleruchies were recovered by Konon in 394-3, in fact Sparta possibly agreed in 392-1 only to recognize a *status quo*; cf. *Hell.* 4,8,15, see also *I.G.* 12,8, p. 3; cf. Wilcken, *Abh. Preuss. Ak.*, no. 15, 1941, p. 4. (The islands were expressly left in possession of Athens in the King's Peace, cf. *Hell.* 5,1,31.)

6. Cf. Wilcken, *Sitzb. Preuss. Ak.* 1927, p. 282; Busolt-Swoboda, 1256, n. 1 (with the additions and corrections of Larsen, *C.P.* 28, 1933, p. 272, n. 50).

7. Cf. Larsen, *op. cit.*, p. 271.

8. Arist. *Ath. Pol.* 23,5; see *A.T.L.* 3, pp. 227, 230; Larsen, *Harv. St. Cl. Phil.* 51 (1940), p. 187; Highby, *Erythr. Decree, Klio* Beitr. 63 (1936), p. 64 sq.

9. Larsen, *C.P.* 28, p. 274; cf. *A.T.L.* 3, p. 232 sq.

10. Cf. Larsen, *op. cit.*, p. 271; Busolt-Swoboda, p. 1325.—For a somewhat similar clause in connection with Athens' relations with her allies cf. the treaty between Athens and the Bottiaean cities of 422 B.C., *I.G.*[2] 90 (= Tod, *Hist. Inscr.* 1, no. 68); Thuc. 7,33,6, treaty between Athens and Thurioi; cf. Schaefer, *Staatsform und Politik* (1932), p. 235; for some later occurrences of the one-sided ἐχθρόν-φίλον formula see, e.g., *SGDI*, 5018, of the second century B.C. (according to Wilcken, *Sitzb.*, p. 282, that was the case also in the treaty of 302 between Antigonos and Demetrios and the Greek cities, *I.G.*[2] 4,68); cf. also Hampl, *Griech. Staatsverträge des 4 Jahrt.* (1938), pp. 59 sqq., and Wᴎᵏen, *Sitzb. Preuss. Ak.* 1929, p. 303.

11. It is as a member of the League that Athens supplies 300 knights for Thibron's expedition (Xen. *Hell.* 3,1,4; cf. Judeich, *Philol.* 81, p. 148); see also *Hell.* 2,4,28; 30; 3,2,25 (cf. Larsen, *op. cit.*, p. 269, n. 40); *Anab.* 6,1,26–7 (cf. Colin, *Xénophon historien*, 1933, p. 29); *Ath. Pol.* 39,2; cf. Wilcken, *Abh. Preuss. Ak.* 1941, p. 6; *Hell.* 2,3,41.

12. The number of ships is mistakenly stated as 10.

13. The explanation applied to the ἐχθρόν-φίλον clause (above, p. 55) does not hold here; π.π. was not among the proposals related by Xenophon, *Hell.* 2,2,11.

14. A detail of clause (a) is preserved in Plut. *Lysan.* 15,2 and Diod. 14,3,6 —it refers to a certain time-limit for the demolition of the Walls envisaged in the treaty (cf. also Lys. 12,74, and Plut. *Lysan.* 15,1).

15. According to Andokides there was a connection between the treaty and the subsequent change of the constitution: φεύγοντας . . . καταδέχεσθαι, τότε ἐπανάγκες, ἐξ ὧν ὁ δῆμος κατελύθη . . . 3,12. That would have been meaningless, had a change of constitution imposed on Athens been known to Andokides; cf. also 1,80; see Meyer, *G.d.A.* 4, p. 666.

16. Cf. Thuc. 4,118 (armistice of 423 between Athens and Sparta); Thuc. 5,18,2 (peace of 421); Thuc. 5,77,5 (peace of 418 between Sparta and Argos); Thuc. 5,79 (symmachy between Sparta and Argos); *I.G.*[2] 2–3,687, 46 (alliance between Athens and Sparta, 266–5 B.C.); *I.G.*[2] 4,68, cf. Wilcken, *Sitzb. Preuss. Ak.* 1927, pp. 277 sqq.; see also Larsen, *C.P.* 20 (1925), pp. 312 sqq.; 21 (1926), pp. 52 sqq., and Cary, *C.Q.* 17 (1923), pp. 137 sqq. (a treaty between Antigonos and Demetrios and the Greek States; the Hellenic League of 302; guarantee of π.π. to the Greek cities); also *I.G.*[2] 1,96,23 (alliance between Athens and Argos of 417–16 B.C.).

17. Cf. preceding note.

18. Smith, *C.P.* 43 (1948), pp. 150 sqq.

19. Cf. Busolt-Swoboda, pp. 1324 sqq. (dating 397–6); see also Parke, *J.H.S.* 50 (1930), p. 53; Munro, *C.Q.* 32 (1938), pp. 19, 21, 23.

20. See Nolte, *Die hist.-polit. Voraussetzungen d. Königsfriedens* (1923), p. 27 sq.; Wilcken, *Abh. Preuss. Ak.* 1941, p. 6; Busolt, *G.G.* 3,2, pp. 1635–6, n. 1; Busolt-Swoboda, pp. 1330 sq., 1337; cf. also Hirzel, *op. cit.*, pp. 54 sqq.

21. Iustin's (5,8,5) 'pacem polliciti si demissa in Piraeum versus muri bracchia deicerent navesque . . . traderent, reique publicae ex semet ipsis 30 rectores acciperent' states explicitly what Lysias wanted his listeners to believe; cf. also Aesch. 2,76.

22. Cf. above, pp. 15 sqq., and especially Jacoby, *Atthis*, pp. 71 sqq., 78 sqq., 114, 122 sq., 131 sq., 294, n. 25, 322, n. 13.

23. *Hermes* 33 (1898), pp. 75 sqq.; cf. also Armbruster, *Hersch. d. Dreissig*, pp. 5 sqq.; Wilamowitz, *Ar. u. Ath.* 1, pp. 123, 288; for a similar view see Judeich, *Rh. Mus.* 74 (1925), p. 260, n. 1.

24. Androtion's work is supposed to have been published shortly after 344–3 (cf. Jacoby, *op. cit.*, p. 1); for the date of Ephoros see Jacoby, *F. Gr. Hist.* IIc, p. 24 sq.

25. The first account of the peace-treaty (Diod. 13,107,4) was apparently taken over by Ephoros from his main authority for the period of the Dekelean war and of the early fourth century (cf. also Barber, *The Historian Ephoros*, 1935, pp. 113 sqq.).

26. The tendency of the source of Diodoros and Aristotle seems to have influenced the chronology, above, p. 59 sq.—A detailed discussion of the chronological problem lies outside my scope. I follow Colin, *op. cit.*; Blank, *Einsetz. d. Dreissig* (1911); Armbruster, *op. cit.*; Beloch 3,2, pp. 204 sqq.; for a different view cf. e.g. Roos, *Klio* 17 (1921), pp. 1 sqq.; Boerner, *De rebus a Graecis inde ab anno 410 usque ad annum 403 a Chr. n. gestis* (1894), pp. 44 sqq.; Busolt-Swoboda, p. 921.

27. It is neither said nor implied in the *Ath. Pol.* that the oligarchs and the democrats propounded their respective ideals under the name of π.π. Such a conclusion seems sometimes to have been arrived at by reading the passage in Aristotle against the background of Diod. l.c.—(I do not discuss here the question whether the moderates were, or were not, organized in ἑταιρεῖαι. Whatever the truth in the version of *Ath. Pol.*, their detachment is intended to reflect credit on them.)

28. Cf. e.g. Barber, *op. cit.*, pp. 88 sqq., 185.

29. To be sure the over-simplification and dramatization in the story might have been due to Diodoros.

30. Munro, C.Q. 32 (1938), p. 24.

31. Ibid.

32. I find Frohberger's article in *Philol.* 14 (1859), pp. 320 sqq., still fundamental (see also Rauchenstein, *Philol.* 15, 1860, pp. 703 sqq.); cf. Blank, *op. cit.*, pp. 45 sqq.; Smith, *Polit. commissions*, p. 79; Meyer, *G.d.A.* 5, p. 19; Colin, *op. cit.*, p. 34 sq. (For a different view cf. e.g. Boerner, *op. cit.*, pp. 75 sqq.; Judeich, *Rh. Mus.* 74 (1925), pp. 254 sqq.)

33. οἱ μὲν ἐν ταῖς ἑταιρείαις ὄντες καὶ τῶν φυγάδων οἱ μετὰ τὴν εἰρήνην κατελθόντες, *Ath. Pol.* 34,3, might be an allusion to the oligarchic forces under the ephors.

34. Cf. e.g. Schwartz, *Rh. Mus.* 44 (1889), pp. 114 sqq.; Blank, pp. 61 sqq.; Frohberger, *Ausg. Red. d. Lys.*[2] (1880), pp. 102 sqq.

35. Cf. Colin, *op. cit.*, p. 36.

36. Lys. 12,71 sqq.; Diod. 14,3,4 sqq., implied in *Ath. Pol.* 34,3.

37. ἕως ὁ λεγόμενος ὑπ᾽ ἐκείνου καιρὸς ἐπιμελῶς ὑπ᾽ αὐτοῦ ἐτηρήθη . . . Lys. 12,71; for this reading cf. Colin, *op. cit.*, 36, n. 1.

38. ὅτι παρασπόνδους ὑμᾶς ἔχοι. That applies most probably to their not having pulled down the Walls; above, p. 80, n. 14.

39. *Die oligarch. Umwälzung* (1841), p. 57.

40. Cf. Breitenbach, *Xen. Hell.* (1884), p. 186 sq.; Underhill, *Xen. Hell.* (1907), p. 28 (*ad loc.*).—The view that the passage in *Hell.* 2,3,2 is an interpolation has been long exploded; cf., more recently, Munro, C.Q. 32 (1938), p. 152.

41. Cf. e.g. Smith, *op. cit.*, p. 80.

42. The constitutional mode of their election is attested also by Isocr. 7,67; Lys. 28,14.

43. Cf. Smith, p. 82.

44. Drakontides appears in Lysias as Theramenes' man (which is incidentally correct); it is Theramenes who is responsible, according to Lysias, for 'Drakontides' constitution'.

45. The hypothesis of Munro, C.Q. 32 (1938), pp. 152 sqq.—that there were two commissions of Thirty, the second (allegedly established according to the 'constitution of Drakontides') divided into three Tens, ruling in turn together with a third of the Three Thousand associated with each—seems to me to be as improbable as it is ingenious.

46. Cf. Kahrstedt, *Untersuch. zur Magistratur in Athen*, 2 (1936), p. 279 sq.

47. The Thirty were, probably, required, as bodies of *syngrapheis* normally were, to submit their constitutional proposals on a specified date; see *Hell.* 2,3,11; *Ath. Pol.* 36,1; Diod. 14,4,2; cf. Smith, *op. cit.*, p. 82.

48. Cf. also Lys. 25,19; Sall. *Catil.* 51,27–31.

49. Cf. e.g. Colin, *op. cit.*, pp. 41 sqq.; Armbruster, *op. cit.*, pp. 30 sqq.

Chapter IV

THE 'CONSTITUTION OF DRAKON'

I TAKE it to be an established fact that the 'constitution of Drakon' related in the *Ath. Pol.* 4 is a later invention, and, consequently, that it is a case in point in the study of the 'ancestral constitution', not a stage in the historical development of the Athenian constitution. In Busolt-(Swoboda), *Staatsk.*, p. 53, n. 2, and 630c–d, references to the works in which 'Drakon's constitution' is regarded as genuine are supplied. I add some references to more recent works in which the genuineness of 'Drakon's constitution' is upheld.[1] A list of contributions in which *Ath. Pol.* 4 is regarded as a later invention is to be found l.c. I add references to some, mainly more recent, discussions [2] and refer especially to the works of Headlam, Ed. Meyer, Wilcken, Bonner and Smith, and, more particularly, that of Ledl (pp. 18 sqq.), for arguments in favour of the thesis that *Ath. Pol.* 4 is an invention.[3]

I propose to discuss here the following questions:

(*a*) the place of *Ath. Pol.* 4 in party-political thought;

(*b*) the date of its origin;

(*c*) the circumstances of its inclusion in the *Ath. Pol.*

There seems to be little agreement with regard to the place of *Ath. Pol.* 4 in the party-political relationship at Athens. To Headlam it reflects the views of a party which looked on Solon as the originator of the changes they deplored, and recommended for Athens a constitution prior to Solon. This view was adopted by Macan and, on the whole, by Ed. Meyer. According to Reinach, ch. 4 goes back to Kritias; while Nissen and Rühl take it to be a forgery by some other pamphleteer of the oligarchic group.[4] According to Wilamowitz, who maintains that the constitution of Drakon is genuine, but owes its transmission to its kinship with the ideas of the late fifth-century opposition, it derives from the group 'around Antiphon and Theramenes'. That is sometimes echoed in later contributions in which the constitution in ch. 4 is dubbed 'oligarchic', though some of its features are recognized as alien to extremist views.

The question was tackled in greater detail by Ledl, and, more recently, by Cloché. According to Ledl, the constitution in ch. 4 is more liberal than that in *Ath. Pol.* 30. Consequently, he takes *Ath. Pol.* 4 to embody the views of the moderates, while *Ath. Pol.* 30 is attributed by him to the extremists.[5] According to Cloché the existence of some democratic elements in *Ath. Pol.* 4 is counterbalanced by certain more liberal features in *Ath. Pol.* 30.[6] Both constitutions originated with the moderate group of the late fifth century.[7]

In view of some lack of clarity, and the prevalent

divergences of opinion, a comparison in some detail of *Ath. Pol.* 4 with the constitutional views of the political parties, more specifically those of the moderates, seems to be required. I take it to have been proved by Ehrenberg and by Ferguson that *Ath. Pol.* 30 is the constitutional advance plan of the Theramenean group, which was fully (or at least in its essentials) realized by them after the fall of the Four Hundred,[8] also that *Ath. Pol.* 29,5, notwithstanding some difference of detail between it and *Ath. Pol.* 30,[9] embodies the basic constitutional principles of the moderates;[10] finally, the *Ath. Pol.* 30 and 29,5 taken together supply fairly full information about the moderate platform.[11] The following comparison is based on these premises.

General principles

(*a*) The basic ruling of the constitution in ch. 4 is the restriction of the franchise to those of hoplite census: ἀπεδέδοτο μὲν ἡ πολιτεία τοῖς ὅπλα παρεχομένοις . . . 4,1 (cf. 4,2). That was the basis of the Theramenean 'polity': τοῖς πεντα-κισχιλίοις ἐψηφίσαντο τὰ πράγματα παραδοῦναι εἶναι δὲ αὐτῶν ὁπόσοι καὶ ὅπλα παρέχονται . . . Thuc. 8,97,1. There is some incongruity in the language used by Thukydides (as well as in the parallel relation of Aristotle, *Ath. Pol.* 33,1: τὰ πράγματα παρέδωκαν τοῖς πεντακισχιλίοις τοῖς ἐκ τῶν ὅπλων). But ὁπόσοι κτλ. leaves little room for doubt that all of the hoplite census were to be included, and the passage is generally taken to mean that there was no numerical

86

restriction of the body-politic in the moderate 'politeia' of 411-10. That is borne out by the fact that in 404 Theramenes was strongly opposed on principle to any numerical restriction of the body-politic.[12] It seems also to be clear from *Hell.* 2,3,48–9—where οἱ δυνάμενοι καὶ μεθ' ἵππων καὶ μετ' ἀσπίδων ὠφελεῖν διατάττειν τὴν πολιτείαν is a paraphrase of ὅπλα παρεχόμενοι—that Theramenes' ideal was rule by all men of hoplite census with no numerical limitation. The occurrence of the term the Five Thousand in Thuc. 8,97,1 (and *Ath. Pol.* 33,1) may be explained by the antecedents of the events of September 411. Thukydides, in describing the situation at Athens on the eve of the revolt, speaks of οὔτε μεθεκτέον τῶν πραγμάτων πλείοσιν ἢ πεντακισχιλίοις 8,65,3. In his description of the assembly at the Kolonos, Thukydides speaks of πεντακισχίλιοι without any qualification, while the corresponding account of Aristotle has μὴ ἔλαττον ἢ πεντακισχιλίοις . . . *Ath. Pol.* 29,5. The correctness of Aristotle's version is confirmed by [Lys.] 20,13 where Polystratos as a cataloguer is said to have put 9000 names on his list. In the story of the rule of the Four Hundred, both in Thukydides and in Aristotle, those entitled to the citizen-rights are uniformly called simply πεντακισχίλιοι,[13] though it seems to be clear that 5000 was the minimum number.

It is sometimes supposed [14] that 'maximum of 5000' reflects the ideas of the extremists, 'minimum of 5000' those of the moderates. However, one of the main causes of the breach between the extremists and the moderates in 411 was the refusal of the oligarchs to institute the Five Thousand. In 404 the oligarchs were forced, under Theramenes' pressure, to establish a body-politic of enfranchized citizens. But they restricted it to 3000, and made it neither stable nor instrumental in the government.[15] It would seem that 'maximum of 5000' was not the ideal of the extremists but their own version of the moderate principle. They were prepared to pay lip-service to this version for tactical reasons but disregarded it when they came to power.[16] In explanation of the fact that the moderates spoke of 'no less than 5000', although they were opposed to any arbitrary numerical restriction, it might be suggested that they meant it in the first place as a suggestion to the *katalogeis* to interpret rather liberally the census qualifications. It is only natural that the name the 'Five Thousand' stuck to the Theramenean body-politic, and it is (somewhat incongruously) used as the name of a body-politic which is to be composed of 'all who could furnish themselves with arms'.

(*b*) The abolition of the democratic *mistophoria* was one of the main principles of the moderate group. In the advance plan it is stressed that the members of the Council are to serve without pay (*Ath. Pol.* 30,2: ἄνευ μισθοφορᾶς, cf. 29,5), and Thuc. reports in 8,97,1 (cf. *Ath. Pol.* 33,1) a full abolition of payments for state service. That is not explicitly stated in ch. 4. However, since 'Drakon's constitution' is based on a property census, since it demands a high property qualification of those who

88

held office, since it envisages fines for non-attendance on the Council (where there is a mistophoria loss of pay comes instead of a fine), use of mistophoria in 'Drakon's constitution' seems to be precluded.[17]

(c) The principle of full rotation in office is adhered to both in the advance plan of the moderates and in 'Drakon's constitution'.[18] The four Councils of *Ath. Pol.* 30 are to rule each for one year, thus comprising the whole body-politic in four years (par. 3: τὸ λαχὸν μέρος βουλεύειν, cf. Thuc. 8,86,3);[19] while ch. 4 envisages that no one might hold office twice until everyone else had his turn.

Similarities of detail

In addition attention may be drawn to the following similarities in detailed arrangements:

(a) The strategoi seem to be the most important officials both in 'Drakon's constitution' (note the high property qualification required of the strategoi in 4,2) and in the advance plan of the moderates (*Ath. Pol.* 30,2; note their priority in the business of the Council, par. 5).

(b) Both constitutions differentiate in a similar manner between the major and the minor magistracies (⟨αί⟩ ἐλάττους ἀρχαί in 4,2—αί ἄλλαι ἀρχαί in 30,2).

(c) 'Drakon's constitution' and the advance plan reveal the same combination of election and lot; the major magistrates are elected (in *Ath. Pol.* 30: ἐκ προκρίτων), the minor appointed by lot (4,2–3; 30,2).

(d) The same age qualification, required for taking part

89

in public life, occurs in both ch. 4 and in ch. 30 (cf. 4,3 with 30,2).

(*e*) The comparatively small property qualification for the archons in 4,2 seems to be paralleled by the salary for them envisaged in 29,5.[20]

(*f*) Fines for non-attendance at the meetings of the βουλή are envisaged both in ch. 4 and in ch. 30 (cf. 4,3, where there are various fines for men of different property classes, with 30,6, where a uniform fine is envisaged). Although such fines are not unknown in Greek political experience [21] they are not attested for Athens' constitutional practice [22] outside 'Drakon's constitution' and the constitution 'for the time to come'.[23]

Differences

(*a*) The most important difference between ch. 4 and ch. 30 is the size and organization of the Council. The advance plan boldly abolishes the two chambers system and envisages four great Councils, ruling in succession, into which the entire body-politic of those of hoplite census is divided. The major magistrates (with the exception of the Hellenotamiai) are included in the officiating Council. This device is highly original, in spite of possible Boeotian influence,[24] and not to be found in ch. 4, which follows the more orthodox pattern of three main bodies: Council (of 401), ekklesia and archai. However, it is an unwarranted assumption of Ledl (*op. cit.*, pp. 32 sqq.) [25] that the ekklesia in ch. 4 is a democratic assembly of all the

Athenians. It is clearly stated at the beginning of ch. 4 that the franchise is restricted (ἀπεδέδοτο ἡ πολιτεία) to those of hoplite census; they are evidently the οἱ ἐκ πολιτείας mentioned later on, and it is never indicated that any rights whatsoever were bestowed on the thetes. It is more likely that the ekklesia in ch. 4 is a general assembly of the ὅπλα παρεχόμενοι.[26] It is worth noting also that the moderate constitution in *Ath. Pol.* 30 envisages a kind of Assembly (or enlarged Council) when it provides that every member of the officiating Council may invite another citizen (i.e. a member of one of the non-officiating Councils) to take part in its deliberations. The main difference between 'Drakon's constitution' and the advance plan would seem, therefore, to be one of organization.

(*b*) Most other differences of detail between ch. 4 and ch. 30 follow from the widely different organizations of the body-politic. The men responsible for ch. 30 are more interested in the Council, and deal with the detailed arrangements of its organization, meetings, and procedure (pars. 3–5), while in ch. 4 comparatively little is said on the working of the Council, but a more detailed account of the magistracies is supplied.[27]

This comparison seems to show that notwithstanding wide differences in organization of the (identical) citizen-bodies of those of hoplite census, the basic principles adhered to in ch. 4 and in *Ath. Pol.* 29,5–30 are identical, and there is a great deal of affinity between their detailed arrangements. They seem to tackle the same basic problem in the same spirit. *Ath. Pol.* 4 is neither more nor less 'liberal' or 'democratic' than *Ath. Pol.* 29,5–30. Both are essentially moderate.

However, the constitution envisaged in ch. 4 bears the name of Drakon, while the late fifth-century moderates used the slogan of a 'return to Solon's and Kleisthenes' ancestral constitution'. That seems to me to be rather an important difference and it is somewhat difficult to explain if we accept the commonly held view [28] that the 'constitution of Drakon' is a party-political forgery concocted in 412–11 (or 412/11–404/3) for propaganda purposes. It is possible that constitutional problems were widely discussed among the Therameneans, and that different solutions concerning the organization of the Council may have been proposed.[29] It seems, however, to be scarcely credible that some members of the moderate group should have conducted their propaganda under the slogan of 'Solon and Kleisthenes', while other Therameneans should use, *at the same time*, and speaking of practically the *same thing*, the name of Drakon.

We shall come back to this difficulty after discussing the date of 'Drakon's constitution'.

(*a*) One of the qualifications for the office of strategos (and hipparchos) is, according to 'Drakon's constitution', that the candidate has sons born in lawful wedlock ($\pi\alpha\tilde{\iota}\delta\alpha\varsigma$ $\dot{\epsilon}\varkappa$ $\gamma\alpha\mu\epsilon\tau\tilde{\eta}\varsigma$ $\gamma\upsilon\nu\alpha\iota\varkappa\dot{\sigma}\varsigma$ $\gamma\nu\eta\sigma\acute{\iota}\upsilon\varsigma$ $\dot{\upsilon}\pi\grave{\epsilon}\varrho$ $\delta\acute{\epsilon}\varkappa\alpha$ $\ddot{\epsilon}\tau\eta$ $\gamma\epsilon\gamma\upsilon\nu\acute{\sigma}\tau\alpha\varsigma$). That is reminiscent of the requirement of the strategoi (and the rhetores) recorded by Din. 1,71. Somewhat similar requirements are suggested in Plato's *Leg.* Rules of this kind [30] are not attested before the fourth century; and Plato might have been influenced by fourth-century legal usage.[31] Furthermore, not only the requirement itself but also the specific sense in which γαμετή is used in our clause seems to point to the fourth-century usage. The question of legitimate birth became rather more acute at Athens in views of Perikles' legislation of 451–50.[32] It recognized as an Athenian citizen only one whose parents were both Athenians (legally married). Thus the μητρόξενοι, who previously had been regarded as citizens, provided that the mother was an ἐγγυητὴ γυνή, were excluded from citizenship. This law was re-enacted in 403–2 and observed thereafter.[33] The formula of introduction of the child to the phratry can be established for the time after 403; it was, normally: ἦ μὴν ἐξ ἀστῆς καὶ ἐγγυητῆς γυναικὸς εἰσάγειν.[34] Some time in the fourth century it became so much taken for granted that the wife had to be an ἀστή (and ἐγγυητή) that a shorter formula came into use. Γαμετή (or γυνὴ γαμετή) sometimes takes the place of both ἀστὴ καὶ ἐγγυητή, or of one of them.[35] It is, I suggest, in this specific sense, evidently characteristic of the fourth-century usage, that it occurs in 'Drakon's constitution'.

(*b*) According to *Ath. Pol.* 4,2 the strategoi and the hipparchoi are to be held to bail by the strategoi hipparchoi and prytanes of the preceding year until their accounts had been audited, taking as securities four men of the same class as that to which the strategoi and the hipparchoi belonged.

Bail is an old institution and is abundantly attested throughout Athenian history (evidence being especially frequent for the period of the developed money-economy in the fourth century). Bailing by members of the same property class is also attested for the fourth century (see the oath taken by the members of the Council in Dem. 24, 144). Guarantee in connection with holding of public office, though well known from papyri and Roman legal sources, does not seem to occur in earlier times except for our passage. It is regarded by Partsch, *Griechisches Bürgschaftsrecht* (1909), p. 395, as a '... Niederschlag fur das juristische Denken des 4. vorchristlichen Jahrhunderts'.[36]

(c) The Council envisaged in *Ath. Pol.* 4 consists of 401 members. Collegia of magistrates of uneven numbers are, of course, not unknown (the Eleven, 9 archons, 51 ephetai). But it is a new device with regard to the Council, which always had been of even numbers (and in fact was bound to be so as it was based on an even number of tribes equally represented); and it is unknown in Athens in connection with large political bodies. The only near parallel seems to be that of the fourth-century law-courts. The weight of evidence is in favour of the view that the fifth-century dikasteria were of round numbers (500, 1000, 1500). The change is attributed to the year of Eukleides, and after 403–2 panels of 501, 201 and 401 occur. The new arrangements were in force by the date of the *Ekklesiazusai*, and occur again in the *Plutos*. Another reorganization, which implied a return to even numbers, took place some time before the date of the *Areopagitikos*.[37] The dikasteria of uneven numbers were at any rate in force for some decades during the fourth century,[38] long enough to impress themselves on the popular mind (note how some of Praxagora's arrangements, *Eccl.* 681 sqq., which have nothing to do with jurisdiction, are influenced by the then prevalent organization of the courts). It seems to me not improbable that the man responsible for 'Drakon's constitution' was similarily influenced by the organization of the law-courts, and that uneven numbers might have appeared to him to be normal.

None of the above analyses could be regarded as establishing the date of ch. 4 conclusively. Combined, however, they seem to show that *Ath. Pol.* 4 reflects some legal and political usages and concepts of the fourth century more than those of any other period, and seem to point to the fourth century as a possible, and even probable, date of 'Drakon's constitution'.

If that be correct I should venture the hypothesis that 'Drakon's constitution' was yet another stage in the fourth-century rivalry for re-interpretation of Athens' constitutional history (cf. above, pp. 7 sqq.). We have already seen how in 411 the moderates tried to claim Kleisthenes for themselves, and that in fourth-century democratic thought, Solon (who seems to have been left to the moderates in the fifth century) becomes the 'father of Athenian democracy'. The general tendency was for each group to delve into the past as deeply as possible in making its own re-interpretation of Athens' constitutional history. It would not, therefore, seem to be too fanciful to suppose that in view of the 'democratization of Solon' in the fourth century the moderates went back yet another step by representing Drakon as an essentially moderate statesman. We should not in this connection think in terms of deliberate actions and counter-actions but rather of general trends pervading the fourth-century tradition of Athens' earlier constitutional history. On this supposition we could regard 'Drakon's constitution' as deriving from a pamphlet comparable to, say, Isokrates' *Areopagitikos*.[39] Such a pamphlet is to be regarded as an invention, going perhaps into more 'historical' detail than the *Areopagitikos*, but hardly as the rather sinister 'forgery' concocted for immediate political use which 'Drakon's constitution' is commonly supposed to be.

As to the question of the inclusion of a chapter on 'Drakon's constitution' in the *Ath. Pol.*, little can be added to Wilcken's (*Apophoreton*, pp. 85 sqq.) main argument. He shows that in the list of constitutional changes given in *Ath. Pol.* 41 'Drakon' hangs in the air between Theseus (No. 2) and Solon (No. 3) with no number given to him, and that the original enumeration had, apparently, been confused by the later insertion of 'Drakon'. Wilcken, arguing back from ch. 41, seems to have made a strong case for suspecting 3,1: ἡ τάξις . . . to . . . τοιάδε, and 7,3: καθάπερ διῄρητο καὶ πρότερον, as later additions to the text

96

consequent on the addition of 'Drakon's constitution'.[40] Wilcken's conclusion is that it is an interpolation by a man from the peripatetic school.[41] His main argument has found wide acceptance, though the view that Aristotle himself was the interpolator, introducing the changes in his original draft after adding to it an account of 'Drakon's constitution', has recently been rather more favoured.[42]

A later addition by, say, one of Aristotle's pupils is not impossible. And, if we suppose that ch. 4 is not a 'forgery', Bonner's objection that nobody would have been sufficiently interested in this insertion does not hold. A pupil of Aristotle might have been misled by a pamphlet on Drakon, and might have found it worth his while to work into the *Ath. Pol.* a description of 'Drakon's constitution'.

Nor is a later addition by Aristotle himself impossible. It is true that when writing *Pol.* 1274, B15, Aristotle did not know of 'Drakon's constitution'. But the pamphlet in which 'Drakon's constitution' was described may have come to his attention in the years between the second book of the *Politics* and the time when the first draft of the *Ath. Pol.* was finished.[43]

I do not see arguments weighing decisively in favour of either of these suppositions. That, however, does not seem to have an immediate bearing on my thesis that the origins of 'Drakon's constitution' are to be sought after not in the party-political clashes of 412/11–404/3 but in the fourth-century political re-interpretation of the constitutional history of Athens.

NOTES TO CHAPTER IV

1. See especially the works of Wilamowitz, Seeck and Lehmann-Haupt quoted there; Warncke, *Die demokr. Staatsidee*, 1951,'38 sqq.; Oliver, *The Athenian Expounders of the Sacred Law* (1950), p. 68; Von Fritz and Kapp, *Aristotle's Constit. of Athens* (1950), 8 sqq.

2. Constanzi, *Riv. Fil.* 29 (1901), pp. 100 sqq.; Verdam, *De Senatu Areopag.*, pp. 21 sqq.; Mess, *Rh. Mus.* 66 (1911), p. 366; Sandys, *Arist. Ath. Pol.*[2] *ad loc.*; Beloch, *Griech. Gesch.* I, 2[2] (1913), pp. 258 sqq.; Smith, *Athen. polit. comm.*, p. 12; Mathieu, *Ath. Pol.*, ed. Budé (1922), p. viii sq.; Freeman, *Solon*, pp. 34 sqq.; Bonner-Smith, *Administr. of justice* I (1930), pp. 134 sqq.; Ehrenberg, *Neugründer d. Staates* (1925), p. 129 sq.; Taeger, *Gnomon* 13 (1937), p. 349 sq.; Munro, *C.Q.* 32 (1938), p. 165; Cloché, *R.E. Anc.* 42 (1940), (Mél. Radet), pp. 64 sqq.; Bloch, *Harv. St. Cl. Phil.*, Suppl. I, p. 352 sq.; Drerup, *Mnemosyne*, 3 ser., 10 (1942), p. 2 sq.; Pearson, *Loc. Hist.*, pp. 23, 159; Schwahn, *P.W. s.v. Theramenes*, col. 2316 sqq.; Jacoby, *Atthis*, pp. 94 (cf. 309 nn.), 123, 154, 268, n. 198, 293, n. 22, 317, n. 140, 347, n. 25, 387, n. 62. Cf. recently Bengtson, *Griech. Gesch.* (1950), p. 110 (Reinach's article in *R.E.G.* 4, 1891, pp. 143 sqq., is still worth mentioning).

3. I quote names only; for details cf. the preceding note, or Busolt-Swoboda, l.c.

4. See also e.g. Ziehen, and, more recently, Freeman, Schlesinger, *C.P.*, 1924, p. 373.

5. This conclusion is mainly based on his view that ch. 4 envisages a popular assembly of all Athenians, not to be found in ch. 30; on the question of the ekklesia cf. p. 90 sq.

6. *Op. cit.*, pp. 70 sqq.

7. See also e.g. Jacoby, Bloch, Constanzi.

8. Cf. Ferguson's note in *C.P.* 21 (1926), pp. 72-5; id. *Mél. Glotz.* I, pp. 349 sqq., and *C.A.H.*, vol. 5, pp. 324 sqq.; Ehrenberg, *Hermes* 57 (1922), pp. 613 sqq.; see Wilcken, *Sitzb. Preuss. Ak.* 1935, pp. 34 sqq. and especially 48 sqq., who adopts most, and works out some, of the conclusions of Ferguson's note.

9. Cf. Kunle, *8 Buch d. Thuc.*, p. 59 sq.

10. Cf. Wilcken, *op. cit.*, 39 sqq.

11. I feel myself unable to share the exceptions taken by Lenschau, *Rh.*

Mus. 90 (1941), pp. 24 sqq.; de Sanctis, *Riv. Fil.* 63 (1935), pp. 205 sqq.; Taeger, *Gnomon* 13, pp. 347 sqq.; for additional support for Ferguson's argument (especially his interpretation of the epigraphical evidence) cf. Meritt, *Classical Studies presented to E. Capps*, pp. 246 sqq.; see also Bloch, *op. cit.*, p. 352.

12. Cf. *Hell.* 2,3,19 with *Ath. Pol.* 36,2 (see also Whibley, *Political parties* (1889), p. 96 sq.).

13. Thuc. 8,72,1; 86,3–6; 89,2; 92,11; 93,2; *Ath. Pol.* 29,5 (end); 31,2; 32,1; 32,3; cf. also e.g.[Lys.] 20,16; Lys. 30,8.

14. Wilcken, *op. cit.*, pp. 35 sqq.; see also Judeich, *Rh. Mus.* 62 (1907), p. 307 sq.; Beloch, *Att. Politik* (1894), p. 4; cf. Ledl, *Stud. ält. Verfassungsgesch.*, p. 33 sq.

15. *Hell.* 2,3,17; 19; *Ath. Pol.* 36.

16. Conversely, *Ath. Pol.* 31 seems to be the furthest the moderates could go out of their way to meet the demands of the extremists. It is a result of a compromise to which the moderates have agreed for the time being. Peisandros' amendment (see Wilcken, *op. cit.*, pp. 38 sqq.) seems to have turned the tables on them. As there is nowhere any reliable evidence that the extremists used the slogan of π.π. or had any 'historical ideal', I suggest taking *Ath. Pol.* 31,1: κατὰ τὰ πάτρια (cf. Stählin, *Hermes* 68, 1933, p. 344) as an indication of the influence of the Therameneans.

17. See also Ledl, *op. cit.*, p. 53.

18. For the differences in its application see p. 90 sq.

19. Cf. also 8,93,2 (a proposal of the extremists to placate the moderates).

20. Cf. Headlam, *op. cit.*, p. 168.

21. Cf. e.g. Arist. *Pol.* 1294A, 37 sqq.; 1297A, 17 sqq.

22. But cf. Plat. *Leg.* 764A.

23. For the Areiopagos cf. above, pp. 21 sqq. (4,2 is regarded by some scholars as the only passage in ch. 4 which might have reflected the conditions of Drakon's time).

24. First recognized by Köhler, *Sitzb. Preuss. Ak.* 1895, pp. 455 sqq. (cf. *Sitzb.* 1900, p. 816); cf. *Hell. Oxy.* 11,3; see also Ehrenberg, *op. cit.*, p. 619.

25. Cf. also Wilamowitz, *op. cit.*, p. 90.

26. Cf. also Macan, *J.H.S.* 12 (1891), p. 27; Rühl, *Rh. Mus.* 46 (1891), p. 446; Seeck, *Klio* 4 (1904), p. 311.

27. The τέλη which are incidentally mentioned in ch. 4, in connection with the fines, do not occur in ch. 30.

28. Cf. note 2.

29. Cf. Cloché, *op. cit.*

30. See also Dem. [59] 92 (where candidates themselves are to be born of γυνὴ ἀστὴ καὶ ἐγγυητή).

31. See Becker, *Platon's Gesetze und d. Griech. Familienrecht* (1932), p. 96 sq.; Chase, 'Plato's Laws and Athenian institutions', *Harv. St. Cl. Phil.* 44 (1933), p. 138.

32. Erdmann, *Die Ehe im alt. Griech.* (1934), pp. 378 sqq.; Busolt-Swoboda, p. 940 sq.

33. Cf. Lipsius, *Das Attisch. Recht und Rechtsverfahren* I (1905), p. 414; Busolt-Swoboda, l.c.

34. Ledl, *Wien. St.* 29 (1907), pp. 198 sqq.; 219; see e.g. Isaeus 7,16; 8,19; Dem. 57,54; Dem. [59] 92; cf. Lipsius, *op. cit.*, p. 470 sq.

35. Cf. Syll.³ 3,921, l. 110: ... ὑὸν ἔναι τοῦτον γνήσιον ἐγ γαμετῆς (the date of this part of the Demotionidai inscription is according to Hiller *v.* Gaertringen, *ibid.*, p. 8, about 350 B.C.; on this inscription cf. especially Wade-Gery, *C.Q.* 25 (1931), pp. 129 sqq.); Is. 12,9, of about 344–3 B.C.: τουτονὶ ὑὸν εἶναι ἑαυτοῦ ἐξ ἀστῆς καὶ γαμετῆς γυναικός. Cf. Wolff, 'Marriage law and family organization in ancient Athens', *Traditio* 2 (1944), p. 68. Γαμετή is used in this sense also in *Ath. Pol.* 17,3; cf. Ledl, *Stud.*, p. 37 sq.

36. To some extent this may be regarded as an argum. e sil. as we know more of fourth-century juridical usage than of that of the fifth. For some technical comment cf. Partsch, pp. 58, 75, 89, 90, 143, 255.—*Ath. Pol.* 4,2 says concerning the strategoi and hipparchoi that they were elected from persons possessing an unencumbered property (οὐσίαν ἐλευθέραν) of not less than ten *mnai*. A somewhat similar requirement is attested for the fourth century by Din. 1,71 quoted above, viz.: γῆν ἐντὸς ὅρων κεκτῆσθαι (where it is coupled, as it is in *Ath. Pol.* 4, with the requirement that the children be born of legal wedlock). Whether the clause in 'Drakon's constitution' applies to land property only, and is consequently to be taken in the sense of 'mortgage', or to property in general, and means in this case 'unencumbered property', cannot be said with certainty. Mortgage is early, for 'unencumbered property' and for the language of our passage we have only fourth-century (and later) parallels: Theophr. in *Stob. Flor.* 44,22; Dem. 35,21 sq.; Syll.³ 364,35, 647,10, 672; cf. also Is. 10,17.

37. See Hommel, *Heliaia* (1927), p. 129.

38. Bonner-Smith 1, p. 243 sq.; Busolt-Swoboda, 1151 sqq.

39. Cf. Ed. Meyer, *Forsch.* I, p. 239.

40. For some further details cf. Wilcken, l.c.; Busolt-(Swoboda), p. 53, n. 2; Bonner-Smith, pp. 145 sqq.; see also Headlam, *C.R.* 5 (1891), pp. 166 sqq.; Macan, *J.H.S.* 12 (1891), 23 sq.; Walker, *C.R.* 8 (1894), p. 206; Meyer, *Forsch.* I, p. 238 sq.; Mess, *Rh. Mus.* 66 (1911), p. 366.

41. He suggests, p. 97, n. 1 (on interpretation of Cic. *de Rep.* II, 1,2), the end of the rule of Demetrios of Phaleron as the terminus ante.

42. Cf. Bonner-Smith, l.c.; Taeger, l.c.

43. It does not necessarily follow that it was then quite recent. Aristotle might well have missed some of the literary productions of this kind. On the question of the dating of the *Politics* and the *Ath. Pol.*, cf. Jaeger, Aristoteles (1923), pp. 275 sqq. and 350; Sandys, *Ath. Pol.*[2], pp. xxi sqq.; xlix sqq.; Keil, *Solon. Verf.*, pp. 190 sqq.

Appendix

THRASYMACHOS, Fr. 1

FRAGMENT 1 of Thrasymachos—preserved by Dionys. Halic. Demosth. 3 as an example of Thrasymachos' style—is the opening of a speech, sometimes called περὶ πολιτείας. Since Thrasymachos was not an Athenian citizen it could not have been a speech delivered by him in the Assembly; it is regarded either as a speech written for some politician's use, or a political pamphlet of the type of Isokrates' *Areopagitikos*, or again a 'symbuleutic model speech'.[1] The text is quoted here by pages and lines of Diels-Kranz, *Vorsokratiker*, II[6].

The first mention of Thrasymachos is in 427 B.C. in Aristophanes' *Daitaleis* (Fr. 198); his Larisean speech must have been written between 413–399 since it is an attack on king Archelaos of Macedonia, and the commonly accepted date for Thrasymachos' life is approx. 460–390. There is no evidence either in the testimonia of Thrasymachos' life or in Fr. 1 itself to enable exact dating of our speech. Its general content, however, and some of the expressions occurring in it may be of some help in establishing an approximate, and tentative, date for the speech.

The term π.π., as applied to Athens' constitution, is not attested before 411; it is sometimes mentioned in middle and late fourth century,[2] but the classic period of π.π. was 411–404/3 B.C. to which belongs the bulk of our evidence. Since c.390 is the latest possible date of the speech the supposition that it belongs to the period 411–404/3 seems to be highly probably. Ὁμόνοια is the other central concept in Fr. 1. It does not occur before the middle of the fifth century.[3] It seems to have been first used by the sophists and in other philosophical literature in ethical and political treatises.[4] The term occurs also in the fourth century, especially in the sense of reconcilement of the Greek states. But the concept of *homonoia* in the specific sense of reconciliation between political factions seems to have been topical mainly in the period 411–404/3 (or 401). When the Athenians in Samos, including the oligarchs, are sworn in by Thrasybulos and Thrasyllos the terms are: ἦ μὴν δημοκρατήσεσθαί τε καὶ ὁμονοήσειν . . . Thuc. 8,75,2. During the clash between the extremists and the moderates in late 411 an Assembly περὶ ὁμονοίας is proposed (Thuc. 8,93,3). The term is used by Aristotle, *Ath. Pol.* 40,3 (cf. Dem. 20,12), to denote the reconciliation of the political parties in 403. It is used in the same sense by Andokides (1,106,109, cf. 76 and 73). And often applied by Lysias to the reconciliation of political parties in 403 (e.g. 25,20,23,27,30; in 21–2 it applies to the two factions among the Thirty), as well as by Isokrates (18,44; 68).[5] The use of *homonoia* in this strictly party-political sense in our speech seems to point again to 411–404/3 as its probable date.⁶ A great political clash over the question of the 'ancestral constitution' is revealed in Thrasymachos' speech. Although this problem might have been topical during the whole of 411–404/3, we know that it was a main political issue of the day in 411 and 404/3 (cf. pp. 1 sqq., 33 sqq., 60 sqq.). There is, however, an indication in our speech which seems to preclude dating it in 404/3. The question of π.π. became for the second time crucial at Athens after the peace-treaty was concluded. The speech of Thrasymachos, however, was written during the Peloponnesian War which is the πόλεμος in p. 323, l. 1.⁷ Athens has exchanged peace for war (p. 323, l. 1–2), and through dangers came to the pitiful state when the woes of the immediate past seemed to be slight in comparison with the ordeals still ahead. That was not the situation in 404/3 when Athens came to have peace instead of war. It seems, however, to fit the situation in the first years of the Dekelean War, about the time when Kleitophon's Rider was proposed.

If this is correct, we learn from Fr. 1 something of the political atmosphere close to the establishment of the Four Hundred. A great political debate is raging at Athens. The question of π.π. is an important point at issue. The parties fight over the π.π. without realizing—Thrasymachos contends—that in fact they speak of very much the same thing. Since there is no reliable evidence that the oligarchs have ever used the slogan of the 'ancestral constitution' (but it was the slogan of the moderates and

104

was sometimes used also by the democrats, for whom the *π.π.* was a democratic regime), the parties here alluded to are to be taken as the moderates and the democrats respectively. 'Ancestral constitution' was to Thrasymachos 'a common good of all citizens' (p. 324, l. 2–3), not a monopoly of any party; and he believed that its nature could be learned both from old men who knew it and from earlier tradition (p. 324, l. 5–6).[8] Thrasymachos does not propound, in the preserved part of the speech, any definite party-political conception of *πάτριος πολιτεία*.

NOTES TO APPENDIX

1. Schwartz, *Comment. de Thrasym. Chalced.* (1892), p. 4; Blass, *Att. Bereds.* 1, p. 250; Jacoby, *Atthis*, p. 386, n. 55; Drerup, ['Ηρώδου] *περὶ πολιτείας* (1908), p. 112; *id., Jahrb. Kl. Phil. Suppl.* 27, p. 227; Wilamowitz, *Ar. u. Ath.* 1, p. 173, n. 76; Schmid-Stählin, 1, 3 (1940), pp. 185 sqq.; Oppenheimer, *P.W. s.v. Thrasymachos*; Diels-Kranz[6], p. 322n.; Köhler, *Sitzb. Preuss. Ak.* 1893, p. 505; *id. Sitzb. Preuss. Ak.* 1895, p. 457, n. 1.; Meyer, *Theopomps Hell.* (1909), p. 259, n. 1; *G.d.A.* 4, p. 577; Busolt, *G.G.* 3,2, p. 1459, n. 4; Beloch, *G.G.* 2,2, p. 377 sq.; Nestle, *Neue Jahrb. Kl. Alt.* 6 (1903), p. 192 sq.; Freeman, *Companion to Pre-Socratic Philosophers*[2] (1949), pp. 376, 380.
2. Cf. above, pp. 8 sqq.
3. Cf. Kramer, *Quid valeat ὁμόνοια in litteris Graecis* (1915), p. 13.
4. Cf. Jacoby (E.), *De Antiph. Soph. περὶ ὁμονοίας* (1908); Kramer, *op. cit.,* pp. 13 sqq., 54 sq.; see also Nestle's remarks in his review of Roller, *Unters. z. Anon. Iamblichi* (1931), in *Phil. Woch.* 1932, col. 1377; Ryffel, *Μεταβολὴ πολιτειῶν* (1949), p. 44 sq.; Aalders, *Mnemos.* 4, Ser. 3 (1950), p. 310; Bock, *Würzb. Jahrb.* 4 (1949–50), pp. 245 sq.
5. Kramer, pp. 19 sqq.

6. Σωφροσύνη (cf. p. 323, l.7–8: ἐσωφρονοῦμεν and σωφρονίζειν) frequently occurs both in ethical and political contexts; although it is not restricted to the period to which Thrasymachos' speech seems to belong (for collection of material cf. de Vries, *Mnemos.* 3, Ser. 11, 1943, pp. 81 sqq.; Kollmann, *Wien. St.* 59, 1941, pp. 12 sqq.) its political topicality in 413–11 (Thuc. 8,1,3; 8,53,3, cf. also the slightly earlier Aristoph. *Av.* 1540) is worth noting.

7. Cf. Blass, p. 258.

8. The former may be perhaps taken to apply to the constitution before the reforms of Ephialtes and Perikles.

CONCLUSION

THERE is no evidence for the use of the slogan of a 'return to the ancestral constitution' in Athenian party politics before 411. The question of πάτριος πολιτεία was, however, one of the main issues of the day on the eve of the revolution of 411.

Kleitophon's Rider, our main evidence in this connection, does not give details of the 'good constitution' the moderates were striving after; we find their detailed proposals, which came shortly after the Rider, in *Ath. Pol.* 29,5 and 30. However, the amendment of Kleitophon indicated the general trend of the moderate thought, which might have developed some time before 411, and their main lines of propaganda. The Rider is tantamount to a rejection of all democratic development later than Kleisthenes. The constitution to be worked out had to take into account the laws of Kleisthenes and the work of Solon. Thus, the Therameneans made a bid for the authority of Solon and Kleisthenes for their constitutional programme; it was to be launched under the name of a 'return to the ancestral polity'.

It seems to me to be likely that the pointed claim of the Athenian democrats at Samos that it was they who wanted to re-establish the 'ancestral laws' abolished by the opposition (p. 33) was a rejoinder to the moderate propaganda conducted under the slogan of a return to the πάτριος πολιτεία. But the clash over the issue of the 'ancestral constitution' was not restricted to such exchanges between Samos and Athens. Thrasymachos' speech shows that a great debate on the 'ancestral constitution' was raging at Athens about the time of Kleitophon's Rider. The extant part of Thrasymachos' speech conveys something of its intensity and of the atmosphere at Athens, though it does not include the arguments used by either side. But, whatever the detailed arguments, the debate must have been in the main on the question of the *true* ancestral constitution—the democrats claiming that it was their democracy, the moderates invoking the name of πάτριος πολιτεία for their constitutional programme, based, allegedly, on Solon and Kleisthenes.

After about four months of the rule of the Four Hundred the extremist supremacy was broken and the moderate *politeia* was established in September 411. Since the moderate programme was first launched under the name of a 'return to the ancestral constitution' it is likely, though not attested, that the new government was inaugurated under the same slogan. It is difficult to determine how far the 'ancestral constitution' was for the moderates a propagandist slogan, and how far they intended to model their polity on that of the past, previous to the democratic developments dating from the sixties of the fifth century onwards. Ideology and propaganda seem to be here mixed up beyond the possibility of disentanglement. If we judge on the basis of the constitutional practice and theory of the moderates as revealed in 412–411 (cf. pp. 86 sqq. with the notes) it must be said that the *politeia* of the moderates was in some respects boldly innovatory, and that there were in it some traits hardly dreamt of by Kleisthenes or Solon (e.g. the Four Councils rotating in office; the fusion of the Council with the Assembly). However, the elimination of the demagogue from political life, abolition of payment for office, abolition of the legislation of Ephialtes and Perikles with regard to the Areiopagos, and above all basing the polity on a property census, would seem to be tantamount to putting back the clock of Athens' constitutional development. Kleitophon wanted Kleisthenes' laws to be studied because this would reveal how far the constitution had moved (in an unfortunate direction) since Kleisthenes. And in fact, when in power, the moderates blotted out democratic developments later than Kleisthenes. Differences of detail (and some democratic influence, e.g. the importance of the strategoi in *Ath. Pol.* 30) apart, the moderates returned, by re-introducing property census, to the past. All in all, the moderate *politeia* of 411–10 would seem to have been basically rather close to Athens' constitutional practice as it was before Perikles.

Democracy was restored shortly after the battle of

Kyzikos, and the democrats firmly established themselves in power in the years 410-5. There was during this period a lull in the open activities of the anti-democratic opposition, and in their propaganda. The return to Athens' constitutional past, if mooted at all during this period, did not leave any traces in the sources extant. The issue of the 'ancestral constitution' returns with the re-emergence of the anti-democratic opposition at the end of the war, and seems to have been crucial in Athenian politics in the years 404-3. It is possible that the moderates were quick to pick on the duplicity of some such phrase as πολιτεύεσθαι κατὰ τὰ πάτρια in the treaty (if there were such a phrase it meant—autonomy) and used it as a pretext to launch again their call for a return to the 'ancestral constitution'. At any rate this call emerges immediately after the peace, and the issue of the 'ancestral constitution' seems to have been even more prominent in party politics in 404-3 than it was ever before. It is in this period that the moderates are to Aristotle specifically the 'men of the πάτριος πολιτεία' as opposed to the democrats and the oligarchs (pp. 65 sqq.). The moderates' agitation for a return to the 'ancestral constitution', which had been going on since the peace-treaty, culminated in the decree of Drakontides, which would seem even more important with regard to the question of π.π. than the Rider of Kleitophon. The Rider was an amendment tabled by the moderates; it indicated to the syngrapheis the moderates' view of the desirability of taking into account Athens' constitutional past when coping with the problems of the present. The decree of Drakontides was a full-fledged constitutional proposal positively enjoining on the new syngrapheis to work out the return to the 'ancestral laws'. The new constitution was to be definitely a return to the πάτριος πολιτεία (p. 75 sq.). There are some indications that steps to implement this clause were being taken in the early, moderate stage of the rule of the Thirty (the outright abolition of the legislation of Ephialtes and Archestratos with regard to the Arciopagos was one of them; pp. 22, 77 sq.). But these attempts were brought to nothing by the extremists' coup d'état.

There is no evidence that the last attempt of the moderates at establishing a polity based on a census—the proposal of the 'πάτριος πολιτεία man' Phormisios (see pp. 40 sqq.)— was launched under the slogan of a 'return to the ancestral constitution'. It is possible, however, that Lysias' περὶ τοῦ μὴ καταλῦσαι τὴν πάτριον πολιτείαν is comparable to the τοὺς πατρίους νόμους καταλύσαντας as used by the democrats in 411 (p. 47 sq.)—i.e. that it was a rejoinder to some such slogan as that of restoring the 'ancestral constitution'. The opening clause of the decree of Teisamenos (pp. 36 sqq.) was, as it were, a symbolic closing-up of the period of the πάτριος πολιτεία clash. It would seem to hint that the 'ancestral constitution' was finally restored—it meant democracy and it had come to stay.

Not for another eighty years was the 'ancestral constitution' a living issue in Athenian party politics (p. 24 sq.) though Isokrates' constant theme of the good-old-times

III

polity of Solon and Kleisthenes sprang directly from the moderates' πάτριος πολιτεία. However, the fourth century was a period of re-interpretation of Athens' early constitutional history, not uninfluenced by some party-political ideas of the late fifth century. Some details of this re-interpretation have been traced in Chapter I (pp. 7 sqq.), and in Chapter IV (p. 95 sq.). It seems that some time during Perikles' rule, Kleisthenes came to be regarded by the democrats as the founder of Athenian democracy. There is no indication before the fourth century that such a rôle was claimed for Solon. The Rider of Kleitophon is the earliest known attempt of the moderates to claim for their programme the authority of Athens' constitutional past. It pointed out that there were in Kleisthenes' work non-democratic elements (in the sense of late fifth-century democracy) on which their constitution could be modelled. And, Solon was claimed by the Therameneans to have been the over-all model for the good constitution which was to be striven after. This view of Solon and Kleisthenes continued in the fourth century with moderate-minded writers. The 'ancestral constitution-theme' of Isokrates; Plut. *Pericl.* 3,2; Plut. *Cim.* 15, 1–3; Androt. *Fr.* 34; Arist. *Pol.* 1273–4 would seem to show that the moderate tradition claimed both the work of Kleisthenes and of Solon to have been basically mixed-moderate constitutions (whatever the terms they chose to call these constitutions by). On the other hand, the democrats went back in the fourth century to Solon. Kleisthenes almost fades away in fourth-century democratic thought; it is Solon whom the democrats claim to have been the founder of Athens' democratic regime (pp. 14 sqq.). The general line seems to have been for each trend to go back as far as possible in re-interpreting Athens' early history. If my suggestion concerning the possible date of the 'constitution of Drakon' is correct it might be regarded as an attempt of one of the moderate-minded writers to go back even further than Solon in party-political, tendentious, interpretation of Athens' constitutional past.

INDEX

(a) NAMES

(b) Sources quoted

117

Herodotos—*cont.*

3,82,5	. .	49 n. 18
5,66,2	. .	25 n. 5
5,67	. . .	25 n. 5
5,69,2	. .	25 n. 5
5,70,2	. .	25 n. 5
5,72,1	. .	25 n. 5
5,73,1	. .	25 n. 5
6,131,1	. .	4

Hypereides

3,21–2	. .	29 nn. 44, 45

I.G.—Inscriptiones Graecae

1^2,71,20	. .	54
1^2,90,18	. .	54, 80 n. 10
1^2,96,23	. .	80 n. 16
$2-3^2$,687,46	.	80 n. 16
4^2,68	. . .	80 nn. 10, 16
12, 8 p. 3.	.	79 n. 5

Isaios

2,13	. . .	29 n. 44
3,42	. . .	29 n. 44
7,16	. . .	100 n. 34
8,19	. . .	100 n. 34
10,17	. . .	100 n. 36
12, 9	. . .	100 n. 35

Isokrates

3,14	. . .	28 n. 28
4,54	. . .	27 n. 21
4,68	. . .	27 n. 21
4,76–7	. .	26 n. 12
4,77	. . .	27 n. 21
5,129	. . .	26 n. 12
7,3 sqq.	. .	28 n. 29
7,13–16	. .	26 n. 12
7,15–30	. .	27 n. 21

7,16	. . .	26 nn. 13, 14, 27
		n. 22
7,20	. . .	26 n. 12
7,21–8	. .	28 n. 28
7,24	. . .	26 n. 12
7,27	. . .	28 n. 30
7,37 sqq.	. .	31 n. 69
7,37	. . .	28 n. 28
7,41–2	. .	27 n. 21
7,44	. . .	27 n. 21
7,47	. . .	27 n. 21
7,50–3	. .	26 n. 12
7,51	. . .	27 n. 21
7,56–9	. .	26 n. 12
7,56–61	. .	27 n. 21
7,57 sqq.	. .	28 n. 29
7,58 sq.	. .	28 n. 30
7,59	. . .	26 n. 13
7,60–1	. .	26 n. 14
7,61	. . .	28 n. 28
7,67	. . .	82 n. 42
7,70	. . .	26 n. 14, 28 n. 29
7, 72 sq.	. .	26 n. 12, 27 n. 21
7,76	. . .	26 nn. 12, 14
7,77 sq.	. .	26 n. 12
7,79 sqq.	. .	26 n. 12
7,153	. . .	27 n. 21
7,197	. . .	27 n. 21
7,312	. . .	27 n. 21
8,4	. . .	26 n. 12
8,12–14	. .	26 n. 12
8,36	. . .	26 n. 12
8,38	. . .	26 n. 11
8,38–56	. .	26 n. 12
8,39	. . .	28 n. 29
8,64	. . .	26 n. 14
8,75–7	. .	26 n. 12